COLIN MONTGOMERIE

THE THINKING MAN'S GUIDE TO

GOLF

The common-sense way to improve your game

COLIN

THE THINKING MAN'S GUIDE TO

MONTGOMERIE
GOLF

The common-sense way to improve your game

TED SMART

Copyright © 2003 Colin Montgomerie

The right of Colin Montgomerie to be identified
as the author of this work has been asserted
by him in accordance with the Copyright,
Designs and Patents Act 1988

First published in Great Britain in 2003 by Orion
an imprint of Orion Books Ltd
Orion House, 5 Upper St Martin's Lane,
London WC2H 9EA

This edition produced for
The Book People Ltd
Hall Wood Avenue,
Haydock,
St Helens WA11 9UL

A CIP catalogue record for this book
is available from the British Library

ISBN 0 75285 372 4

Designed by Harry Green
Printed in Italy by Printer Trento srl

Contents

Foreword

John Jacobs is one of the most revered individuals ever to grace the European game. As a player of considerable repute, he won several international titles and in 1955 represented Great Britain and Ireland in the Ryder Cup in Palm Springs. Once he hung up his clubs he became a tournament director at the PGA and was one of the leading lights in the setting up of the PGA European Tour in 1971. He also captained two European Ryder Cup teams, first in 1979 and again in 1981. However, it is as a teacher that he may well be best remembered. Sometimes called 'Dr Golf' or 'the Godfather of the Gurus', it is no exaggeration to suggest he is one of the architects of the modern golf swing. Jacobs was awarded the OBE for his services to golf in the Queen's Birthday Honours List in 1997. Three years later, he was inducted into the World Golf Teachers Hall of Fame. He writes:

ALTHOUGH COLIN has occasionally sought my opinion, I don't believe I have influenced his game in any way. He rightly pays tribute to Bill Ferguson, who so importantly got him off to the right start, and latterly Denis Pugh, whose friendship and advice will have been of help more recently. However, I think all would agree that Colin's huge success has been very much self-generated. I confess that I wondered, 'Why me?' when asked to write this brief foreword. Once I had studied the manuscript, though, I came to the conclusion that it could well be appropriate for me to contribute this foreword since I have so much in common with the content of the text.

Firstly, there is the fact that Colin has been able to introduce simplicity into what is a most comprehensive study of how to play this very difficult but wonderful game.

And secondly there is the recognition that there are varying ways of swinging the club: something which is very dear to my heart is the assertion that so long as the swing provides for a correct and repetitive impact, the specific may vary considerably. As my dear mother used to say, 'There are many ways of making good pastry.'

The fundamentals of grip, club face, aim, body alignment and posture are rightly given prominence in the book, since they are the elements that have such a direct bearing on the subsequent ability to arrive at the correct impact, and, in turn, the desired ball flight.

How different situations confronting us on the course are dealt with should be of immense help to players at all levels. To visualise the type of shot required and to understand what the club must do at impact is always going to help turn good hitting into good scores.

Colin's wonderful Ryder Cup record may tell us a little about his temperament – playing in a team does away with dwelling on the putt that lips out or an unfair bad bounce. If this positive approach can be applied when competing for a much coveted Major, it may well lead to success. No one has come closer or striven harder or deserves a Major more than Colin, and it would be to the greatest delight of his huge army of admirers and supporters if the title of his next book read *There at Last*.

JOHN JACOBS

What This Book

Over the years, I have made no secret of the fact that I believe I could save an average golfer about six or eight shots a round if I got the opportunity to caddie for him. It is not something I have tested in real life, I grant you, but I do believe it to be true and would welcome the opportunity to explain why.

In my experience, gathered playing in literally hundreds of pro-ams, I have found that amateurs often drop shots, not because they make poor swings, but because they make bad mental errors. I have lost count of the times I have watched amateurs run up ruinous eights or nines, not because they have hit one downright bad shot, but simply because they have attempted to hit the wrong shot at the wrong time.

A couple of years ago, for example, I happened to be paired with a senior business executive in a pro-am staged over the Brabazon course at the Belfry, the scene of Europe's most recent Ryder Cup triumph over the Americans. Clearly, given his lofty position, he was a man used to making decisions based on sound business principles but, for whatever reason, that ability to think logically, analytically, seemed to go out of the window as soon as he stepped foot on the first tee.

That day this 18-handicap golfer hit the ball pretty well, at least by his own standards, but I doubt that he broke 100 simply because he hit one downright daft shot after another. On the fourth, for example, he ran up a ten, having driven into the trees and then attempted an impossible shot out through a minuscule gap in the foliage. Later, on the eighteenth, if I recall, he lost three balls, attempting a carry over the water that I might not even have taken on.

is All About

That, I should add, was by no means an isolated experience. Over the years, I have lost count of the times I have watched amateur partners get into all sorts of trouble, either by attempting the impossible or not thinking through the shot at all.

Sitting down to write *The Thinking Man's Guide to Golf*, I was conscious of the fact that it was part of my remit to give the reader good, basic advice on how to swing a club because, without such information, no one would ever be able to get round a golf course. Equally, however, I did not want to stop there because that would mean leaving out arguably the most important thing I have learned over the years, namely that to become a good golfer you have to think your way around a golf course.

I remember, a few years ago, watching a young Swedish golfer hitting some shots. He had a marvellous swing, and hit the ball exceeding well, so much so that I turned to his coach and told him how good I thought his pupil looked. 'He does hit the ball well,' replied the coach, before adding, somewhat ruefully, 'but I'm afraid he's still not much of a golfer.'

To me, that is an important distinction, but one that is often overlooked, even by experienced players who, one would have thought, should know better.

Over the years, I have learned that to become a successful golfer, it is not enough just to hit the ball well. You have to learn how to scramble, to get up and down when you miss a green and, above all else, learn to hit the right shot at the right time. Put in simple terms, you have to learn how to manage your game, something I hope this book will help you to achieve.

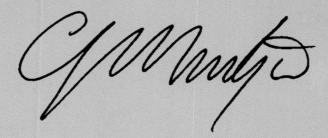

Like a lot of other Scottish children, I did not have to look far to find a golf course. For the first three and a half years of my life, I lived in Troon, where my father, James, was the secretary of Royal Troon, and it was there, on the little practice course next to the ladies' club, that I began to play the game.

How I Got Started at Golf

I wish I could report that, like Tiger Woods, I was a child prodigy, but, in all honesty, I cannot. In those days, I did little more than potter round this little nine-hole course with my brother, Douglas, but it was enough to get me interested. I was four, and Douglas was six, when my father got a new job in Ilkley, and it was there, a couple of years later, that I had my first lesson, from Bill Ferguson, the local club professional.

At that time, Bill, or Mr Ferguson as he was to me, was the National Club Professional champion. He was a hugely respected figure, both at Ilkley and beyond, so when he told me that my left-hand grip was far too strong I knew I had to listen. Over the next few years, Bill was largely responsible for turning me into a golfer. My father, a single-figure amateur, helped me a bit, but it was Bill who made the biggest contribution, forming the basis of the swing I still use today. Nowadays, if you look at the old pictures of me, you will see that the swing I developed as a nine-year-old is remarkably similar to my current swing. In many respects, particularly my leg action, the likeness is uncanny. The follow through is also instantly recognisable. It would be wrong to suggest that my swing back then was the finished article, but it is clear that Bill gave me a wonderful grounding.

At that time, golf played a relatively minor role in my life. In fact, apart from holiday and weekend golf with Douglas and my parents, I did not play much in my young days at Ilkley. The reason for this was that for most of the year I lived at Strathallan, a public school in Perthshire, Scotland, where golf was encouraged much less than it is today. At Strathallan, the main sports were rugby, hockey and cricket. In the winter, we played rugby for a term and a half and then hockey for half a term. In the summer, cricket dominated, just as it did at all public schools in the 1970s. The end result of playing all those other sports was that when I left Strathallan, my handicap was no better than six.

I was a long way from being a complete golfer, but I had posted the odd sub-70 round from time to time, and that fact would prove crucial when persuading my father to allow me to embark on what turned out to be virtually two years of full-time amateur golf. Fortunately for me, my father recognised natural talent when he saw it, and agreed that I should give it a go. At that time, living in Yorkshire, it would have been far easier for me to play on the English amateur circuit, but, as a Scot, and a proud one at that, I chose to head north instead. I never regretted that decision, then or now.

Playing on a full-time basis, my golf soon started to improve. In 1982, I finished third behind Stephen Keppler at the British Youths Championship, a performance that was probably instrumental in my receiving a first Scottish Youth cap the following year. Then, in September 1983, armed with my clubs, I crossed the Atlantic to embark on a golf scholarship at the New Mexico Military Institute. In those days, the collegiate circuit in the States attracted far fewer British youngsters than it does now, but I was adamant it would improve my golf. However, within a couple of days, I realised military life was not right for me. Luckily, Dave Mannen, the respected coach at Houston Baptist University, came to my rescue. He could not give me a golf scholarship because the term had started and all the places had been filled, but he did agree to take me, in a 'walk-on' capacity, thereby giving me the opportunity to show that I was worthy of a scholarship the following year.

Nowadays, looking back, it is easy to see what four years in Houston did for my game. Playing on uniform courses, I soon developed into a much more consistent performer, which was just as well, because there were a great many good golfers around at the time, including Billy Mayfair, Davis Love, Steve Elkington, Duffy Waldorf and Scott Verplank, to name just a few. Dave Mannen also turned out to be an excellent coach.

The combination of courses and coach worked wonders. When I left home in September 1983, I was what could be described as a promising youngster. Within months, I moved up to a different level altogether, something that was obvious from my results. While at Houston I won ten collegiate titles and invariably played at number one or number two on the team. At home, during the holidays, I also made my mark. In the summer of 1984, for example, on my first vacation from Houston, I finished runner-up to José María Olazábal at the Amateur Championship at Formby. Over the next three years, I went on to win the Scottish Stroke Play Championship and the Scottish Amateur Championship, capping my amateur career with two appearances in the Walker Cup, in 1985 and 1987. The time had come to turn professional and see if I could earn a living from the game.

The records show that in 1987, having turned pro after the Walker Cup, I played in three events, winning less than £2,000. However, the following year I fared much better, claiming 52nd place on the European Tour Order of Merit and succeeding the likes of Tony Jacklin, Bernard Gallacher, Peter Oosterhuis, Sam Torrance and Olazábal as the Sir Henry Cotton Rookie of the Year.

That, of course, was just the start for me. In 1989, I won my first Tour title, finishing eleven shots ahead of the field at the Portuguese Open at Quinta do Lago. In 1993, I captured the first of my seven consecutive Order of Merit titles. Altogether, to date, I have won twenty-seven times in Europe, with more to follow, I hope. I have also represented Europe in six Ryder Cup sides, being on the winning team three times, most recently in 2002.

If I tell you that I can remember virtually every shot I have hit in a Ryder Cup, you may get some idea of how much this biennial contest means to me. Those Ryder Cups have provided me with many fond memories, often stemming from my singles tussles against the likes of Scott Hoch (twice), Payne Stewart, Ben Crenshaw, Lee Janzen and Mark Calcavecchia. I love the cut and thrust you get in singles match play, which might go some way to explaining why, in six singles to date, I remain undefeated, having claimed four victories and two halves. It was a particularly great honour to lead Sam Torrance's team out during the last match at the Belfry, and I'd like to think my 5 & 4 victory over Hoch helped to set the tone for that historic afternoon. That Ryder Cup was the ultimate for me. Were I to win each of the Majors in turn, and I'd love to, I doubt I'd enjoy myself as much as I did during that week in September.

I have worked hard at my game in order to be a participant in weeks like that. But I have also been fortunate, not just to be born with natural talent, but also to be the recipient of such great advice from a whole host of people. As I sit down to write this book, I am conscious that I owe thanks to a lot of people without whom I would not have succeeded. These include my father, Bill Ferguson, Dave Mannen, Denis Pugh, Hugh Mantle and others. They have been a huge help to me over the years and I owe them a huge debt of gratitude.

This book contains many of their ideas and techniques, but also my own thoughts on a game that is sometimes euphoric, sometimes infuriating. It is a distillation of everything I have learned from coaches and from my own experience. Hopefully, it will help you become the best golfer you can be.

Like most Tour professionals, I spend most of my time playing golf rather than teaching it. However, I am not completely new to coaching. Far from it, in fact, because not only have I tried to help literally hundreds of amateurs during pro-ams, but I have also played an active part in numerous more structured sessions at the Colin Montgomerie Links Golf Academy at the Westin Turnberry Resort in Ayrshire, Scotland.

A couple of years ago, I was delighted to form a partnership with Starwood Hotels and Resorts through which we developed The Colin Montgomerie Links Golf Academy at Turnberry, and I can honestly say that I have thoroughly enjoyed the association. Obviously, my Tour schedule and other activities restrict my visits, but, when there (about six times a year), I like nothing better than to put my teaching theories into practice.

Sometimes at Turnberry, I give clinics for corporate groups. At other times, I coach individual members of the public. However, whatever the audience, I try to get across the message that golf is a relatively simple game, often made more complicated than it really should be. That, in a nutshell, is what my academy and this book are all about.

The only difference between the academy and the book is that the former concentrates predominantly on teaching the art of links golf, while the latter is expanded to deal with golf in all its forms. To me, links golf is the purest form of the game, and the most enjoyable, too. I suppose I am biased, having been brought up by the seaside, at Troon on the west coast of Scotland, but I genuinely believe that there is nothing better than to set out on a links course with a hint of breeze in the air. Over the eighteen holes, you will be required to hit high shots, low shots and all sorts of shots in between. Sometimes you will be the victim of bad bounces, but that is something you have to accept, however hard it may be to do so.

Earlier, I stated that I learned to be a consistent ball striker on the American collegiate circuit. However, it was at home in Scotland where my views on golf and my golf swing started to develop. Put together, they make me the golfer I am today.

THE COLIN MONTGOMERIE LINKS GOLF ACADEMY

PART 1 THE LONG GAME

I have always thought that assembling a golf swing is a bit like building a house: the foundations are crucial in both. Get the foundations wrong when building a house and it will collapse almost as soon as it has been erected. Ignore the basics in golf and the results will be almost as catastrophic.

Getting the Basics Right

It's impossible to overestimate the importance of a sound grip and a solid set-up in the game of golf, which is why I decided to start *The Thinking Man's Guide to Golf* with a chapter devoted to them. It is a chapter that no golfer can afford to ignore if he harbours hopes of playing consistently, and it forms the basis for everything else that I move onto later in the book.

Since turning professional back in 1987, I have played in hundreds of pro-ams, alongside countless amateurs of differing ability. Some, of course, have played highly proficiently, but many others have struggled, invariably, or so it seems to me, simply because they have got the basics wrong. The simple fact of the matter is that, whether you slice the ball, hook it or whatever, the chances are the problem stems from getting one or more of the basics wrong. That, in turn, sets off a chain reaction, leading, inevitably, to one poor shot after another.

Whatever your problem, I recommend that you should review your grip, your posture and your set-up before looking at anything else, as these are the sources of almost all swing faults. Even if you are fortunate enough to hit the ball consistently, it makes sense to review the basics from time to time, as you can easily slip into bad habits without realising that you have.

GRIPPING STUFF

It is impossible to exaggerate the importance of a good grip. Grip the club correctly, and you have a chance to develop into an accomplished golfer. Get it wrong, and you will never reach your full potential.

Right from the start, Bill Ferguson, my first coach at Ilkley, impressed on me the importance of having a good grip. To this day, I still remember going to him for my first lesson and being told that I would never be a good golfer unless I 'weakened' my grip. Fortunately, I listened to his advice because, without it, I doubt I would ever have won a club monthly medal, let alone seven consecutive European Tour Order of Merit titles.

When you start to play golf, the first priority is to build a grip that enables you to return the club square to the target at impact. Because we are all individuals, each and every one of us will find a slightly different way of doing that, but, make no mistake, returning the club square at impact has to be the primary goal for all of us.

Over the years, the golf grip has evolved, but, nowadays, there are three basic types of grip: the interlocking grip (opposite page), the overlapping grip (above left) and the two-handed grip (above right). Since my days at Ilkley, I have used an interlocking grip, simply because it feels most comfortable, but you might want to experiment to see which one works best for you.

PUTTING THE LEFT HAND ON THE CLUB

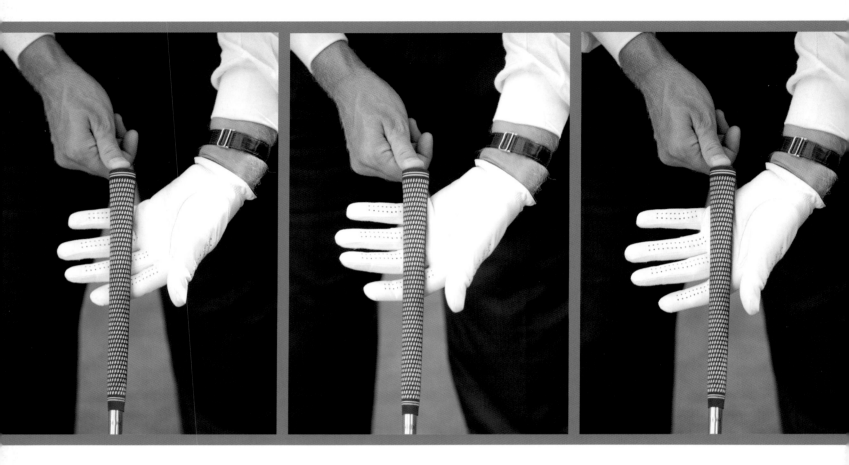

The left hand provides the control during the golf swing. Most PGA professionals will tell you that you should place the club across the base of the fingers as this gives the best combination of power and control (above left). I am somewhat different in that I tend to grip the club a little higher in my palm (above centre), but that is a personal preference and might not be right for you. The one thing you must avoid is placing the grip too much in the palm of your hand (above right), as that will create tension and cut down your ability to create club-head speed.

Once you are confident the grip is nestling in the base of your fingers, simply wrap your hand round the grip, ensuring that the 'V' created between the thumb and forefinger is pointing between your chin and right shoulder.

When gripping with the left hand, you should feel as if you are holding the club solidly, but not rigidly, between the last three fingers and the fleshy pad at the base of your thumb.

ADDING THE RIGHT HAND

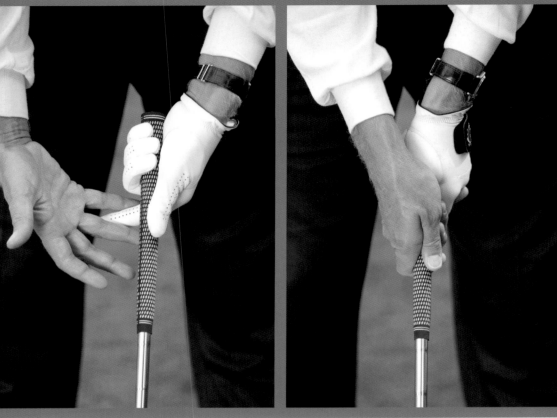

The right-hand grip sits more in the fingers than is the case with the left-hand grip. I hold the club securely, but not tightly, with my middle two fingers and with the pad below my right thumb nestling on the top of my left thumb.

In golf, you want your hands to work as a unit. For that reason, the two hands should be parallel, with the 'V' created between your right thumb and right forefinger pointing more or less in the same direction as the 'V' on your left hand. As with the left hand, be careful not to grip too tightly, as this creates tension and cuts down club-head speed. During the swing, you want your hands and arms to feel relaxed, not rigid, and this is impossible if you have a stranglehold on the club.

COMMON GRIP FAULTS

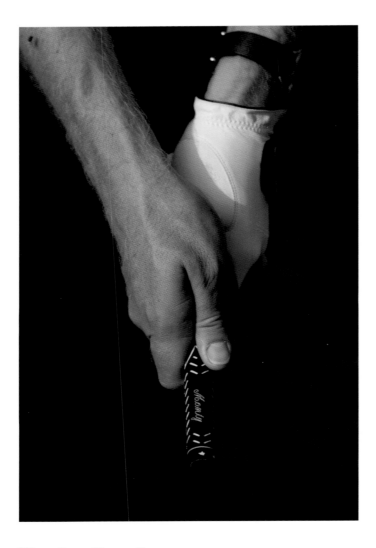

WEAK LEFT-HAND GRIP

If your left-hand grip is weak, you will see only one knuckle on your left hand (see above). This causes serious problems because, the weaker your grip is, the less forearm rotation you will have, and the harder it will be for you to square the club at impact. To correct this fault, move your hand over to the right so that you can see two, or two and a half, knuckles. The 'V' formed between your thumb and forefinger will no longer be pointing at your chin, but midway between your chin and your right shoulder.

If you are struggling to get the left hand in the correct position, try gripping the club with your left arm hanging at your side. In this position, the left hand and forearm naturally hang inwards, in a strong position.

WEAK RIGHT-HAND GRIP

This is another classic grip fault, one I see a lot during pro-ams (see above). Here, the right hand is turned much too far to the left, or on top of, the grip. It might feel secure, but it is actually a weak position that makes it difficult for the golfer to release his hands properly through impact. The solution is to move the right hand into a more neutral position, with the 'V' formed between your thumb and forefinger pointing between your chin and your right shoulder.

HANDS WORKING
AGAINST EACH OTHER

I would argue that somewhere between 80 and 90 per cent of all amateur golfers have a grip problem. In a good grip, the hands should be parallel, enabling them to work together (see right). However, all too often, this does not happen. Instead, they fight against each other. The result is that the wrists cannot hinge properly on the backswing. The elbows break instead, resulting in a short and extremely weak movement.

THE KEYS TO A SOUND SET-UP

Once you are gripping the club properly, the next thing to do is to make sure your set-up is right. Like the grip, a good set-up is vital. Get in the right position, and you can make a sound swing. Get it wrong, however, and it is highly unlikely that you will hit more than the occasional good shot.

1 Bend forward from the hips, keeping your back relatively straight. At 6' 1", I am slightly more bent over than I would be if I were under 6'.

2 At address, the shoulders should be nice and relaxed. They should not be hunched forward or pushed back unnaturally as that would create tension and restrict movement.

3 A good tip is to feel as if the upper arm is resting on the side of the chest, just here.

4 The arms hang down directly from the shoulders. Because of their height, tall golfers stand relatively close to the ball, and swing fairly upright. Smaller golfers stand further away and swing more flat.

5 Note that my hands are arched slightly upwards. If they are too low, that will result in too much wrist action in the swing. As a general rule, when in the address position, the butt of your club should point directly at your belt buckle.

6 Flex your knees just enough to feel balanced and athletic. Taller players need slightly more knee flex, shorter ones slightly less.

7 The weight should be on the balls of your feet, not on the toes or the heels. Except for a special shot, like a punch, the weight should be distributed evenly between the feet.

COMMON POSTURE FAULTS

CHIN TOO LOW

It is all very well keeping your head down during the swing, but you do not want to overdo it (see above). Instead, you should ensure that your chin is high, giving your left shoulder plenty of room to turn under it on your backswing.

BACK TOO STRAIGHT

At address, you should bend forward a little from the waist, giving your arms room to swing past your body. When your back is too straight (see above), this movement will be restricted.

TOO MUCH KNEE FLEX

Most golfers know they have to flex their knees but some tend to bend them too much (see above). This is a serious problem because it will restrict your ability to turn your shoulders, thereby limiting the distance you hit the ball.

TOO LITTLE KNEE FLEX

Here, the problem is too little, not too much, knee flex (see above). If you do this, you will tend to lock your legs, which can lead to a loss of balance and will also result in a loss of power.

THE VIEW FROM THE FRONT

Because you grip the club with your right hand below your left, at address your right shoulder will automatically sit lower than your left. This helps you to stand with your head a little behind the ball where it should remain through impact. It also helps you to swing the right shoulder down and under rather than over and around when coming through.

When hitting a wood, I stand with my feet about shoulder width apart. If your stance is narrower than that, you will struggle to maintain your balance. Any wider and you will restrict your shoulder turn on both the backswing and the follow through. With the shorter irons, the stance can be a little narrower because you are generating much less club-head speed.

My left arm is straight, but not stiff. The right arm feels a little 'softer', my right elbow pointing to my right hip.

My left foot is turned out about 30 degrees but my right foot is almost square. The position of my feet is important. Keeping the right foot almost square helps me to keep my weight on the inside of that foot during the backswing. My left-foot position allows me to transfer my weight easily through impact.

HOW TO GET YOUR POSTURE RIGHT EVERY TIME

A good way to find out what a sound address position feels like is to try this simple three-part drill.

1 Start by standing up straight with your club pointing straight up in the air (as shown). Your arms should be just above your belt buckle, and your elbows by your sides.

2 The next thing is to bend forward by sticking out your bottom, keeping your back straight. Note that your club shaft should still be in the position shown.

3 Now drop your arms until the club head hits the ground.

This drill will not only let you experience what good posture feels like, but will show you how far the ball should be from your feet with every club in the bag.

GET YOUR BALL POSITION RIGHT

I believe that ball position should change depending on what club you are hitting. When I have a driver or a fairway wood in my hands, I position the ball just inside my left heel. With a 5-iron or one of my other medium irons, it will be midway between the left heel and the centre of my stance. When hitting a wedge or another short iron, it is even further back, virtually in the middle of my stance.

I change the ball position for a reason. When you are hitting one of the short irons (up to about the 7-iron), you want to deliver a slightly descending blow, one that creates backspin, and you have to move the ball back in the stance to achieve it. With the medium irons, however, the aim is to make contact with the ball when the club is at its lowest point of the swing arc, so the ball has to be slightly forward, towards your left foot. Finally, with the driver, the idea is to sweep the ball away, so it is even further forward in the stance.

KEEP YOUR HANDS A CONSTANT DISTANCE FROM YOUR BODY

Looked at from a different angle, you will see that when I am using a driver the ball will be a good bit further from my body than it is when I am hitting a medium or a short iron. This is not the result of a conscious decision on my part, but is simply because woods have the longest shafts, and the wedges have the shortest.

The distance between my feet and the ball changes from club to club, but one measurement that never alters is the one between my hands and my thighs. If you watch golf on TV, you will see this gap varies from player to player. However, watch each player closely and you will see it does not change from shot to shot.

SET YOURSELF TO THE TARGET

All too often, amateur golfers are so keen to hit the ball they forget to take proper aim. Unfortunately, that is a bit like firing a rifle without homing in on where you want the bullet to go, and the result is invariably the same — the shot misses the target.

In contrast, Tour professionals tend to make a ritual out of taking aim because they know how important it is. Almost to a man, we have a pre-shot routine we go through every time we hit a shot. We never deviate from it because we know that if we do, we will not be properly prepared to pull the trigger.

When a good golfer is going through a bad spell, the first thing he will do is check that his set-up is right. More often than not, without him knowing, he will have slipped out of position slightly, meaning that he has to make subconscious swing changes to compensate. The poor player, in contrast, seldom gets into a good address position, except by accident, which explains why he seldom hits good shots.

Either way, the problem has to be rectified because, if you do not get your set-up right, you will never achieve consistent results. It's as simple, and as important, as that.

PREPARE YOURSELF FOR THE SHOT

PICK A SPOT

Many golfers find it difficult to line up to a target 200 yards, or more, in the distance. If you are one of those, why not select an intermediate target and aim at that instead? After all, if it works for Jack Nicklaus, then it should work for you, too.

Nicklaus and others pick a spot on the ground three or four feet in front of the ball, directly in line with the target, and then line up to it. It might be a weed, a divot, or whatever. It does not really matter, provided it is exactly in line with where you want the ball to go.

Once I have selected the club, I go through a five-part routine designed to ensure that I am prepared to hit the shot. First I stand behind the ball and focus on my exact target. It is not enough just to have a vague target in mind: you need an exact picture in your mind of where you want the ball to go. Whenever possible, I will pick out a specific target, a tree, a bush, a flag, whatever. That remains the focal point right until I hit the shot.

REHEARSE WHAT YOU WANT TO DO

Having got a picture of my target in my mind, the next step in my routine involves practice swings. If I plan to do something out of the ordinary, like hit the ball from right to left, I will rehearse the moves I need to make to achieve that shape of shot. If not, I will simply make a couple of leisurely practice swings, being careful to complete the swing just as I will do when I hit the ball.

LINE UP YOUR CLUB HEAD

The next stage involves lining up the club head before moving your body into position, not the other way round, as a lot of golfers do. The problem with lining up the body first is that it is extremely difficult to get into the correct position, square to the target. It is much easier to aim the club head first and then move your body into position relative to it.

To get the club head into the correct position, you need to ensure that the bottom edge of the club is at a right-angle to the target. When you are doing this, you need to be as precise as possible because, if the club face is not lined up properly, the chances of hitting the ball on target are vastly reduced.

MOVE YOUR BODY INTO POSITION

When I am aligning the club head, my right foot will be close to its final position, but my left foot will be almost behind it, well

out of the way. Next, I move my body into position, ensuring that my shoulders, chest, hips, knees and feet are all square, or parallel, to the club face. In my case, all will be pointing slightly to the left of where I want the ball to finish. That is because I hit the ball naturally left to right. If, on the other hand, you draw the ball, you will aim slightly right to allow the natural curve of the ball to bring it back on target.

WAGGLE AND LOOK BEFORE YOU GO

Once in position, I make a couple of waggles, not to rehearse a swing move, like Masters champion Mike Weir or former US Open champion Corey Pavin, but simply to help me to relax and get a feel of the club head.

Finally, I take one last look at the target, taking great care not to move out of position as I do it. Then, and only then, am I ready to hit the shot.

Readers need only watch the top stars in action
to realise there is no such thing as one way to swing
a golf club. Over the years, all the leading players
have perfected their own individualistic methods
of hitting the ball, albeit while adhering
to a common set of principles that has to be
adopted in order to play well.

Putting the Swing Together

In this chapter I will show you all the basic moves that are needed to build a consistent swing. But first it is worth stressing just what it is you should be trying to achieve when you swing a golf club.

It was that great teacher John Jacobs who stated that the sole purpose of a golf swing was to 'move the club through the ball square to the target at maximum speed', and he was quite right. It matters little how you achieve this goal, only that you build a swing that allows you to do it, time and time again.

My own swing is a good example of how this works in practice. It could not be described as classical, in the mould of a Sam Snead or a Tom Weiskopf, but it is technically sound, consistent and enduring.

What follows is some advice on how you can build your own solid, repeatable swing, one that enables you to hit more good shots than you have ever done before. But, remember, that is only half the battle. Mastering golf is not just a mechanical exercise. It also requires common sense, intelligence and clear thinking, attributes that we will address in later chapters.

TAKE THE CLUB BACK LOW AND SLOW

Once you have got yourself into a good address position (see above), the next step is to start the swing with a leisurely one-piece movement of the shoulders, arms and hands. For me, the key is to concentrate on taking the club back 'low and slow', the club tracking back close to the ground for the first eighteen inches or so.

When starting the swing, it is important not to jerk the club back as this will affect your rhythm during the rest of the swing. Instead, concentrate on taking the shoulders, arms and hands back slowly, as a unit, being careful to ensure that your arms and body are in sync throughout the movement.

In the past, you might well have heard coaches talking about taking the club straight back from the ball. This is sound advice, but requires some clarification. Because you are standing to one side of the ball, what actually happens when you initiate a one-piece takeaway is that the club moves straight back for a couple of inches and then tracks inside a little. This is inevitable and should be allowed to happen. Certainly, you should not attempt to keep the club moving straight back for longer than feels natural, as this would mean the hands and arms would have to work independently of the body. Equally, however, you should not attempt to roll the wrists and move the club onto an inside line, as this would also destroy the one-piece movement and lead to problems later.

MAINTAIN THE ONE-PIECE MOVEMENT UNTIL HALFWAY BACK

When starting the backswing, it is a good idea to try to maintain the triangle formed by your arms and chest for as long as possible. If you make a good one-piece takeaway the triangle will still be intact as the club passes parallel (see above). Your shoulders should have started to turn and your weight will be moving onto your right side. Note that my right knee is still flexed, just as it was at address. That is a position that should be maintained throughout the backswing.

COILED LIKE A SPRING

Here, at the top of my backswing, I have achieved my main objective: namely, to get myself into a good position to hit down, and through the ball. At the top of the backswing, your shoulders should have turned 90 degrees but your hips only 45 degrees, giving you the feeling that you are coiled like a spring.

My coach, Denis Pugh, talks about turning your upper body behind the ball in the backswing. He wants you to feel that you are getting your left shoulder over and above your right thigh at the top of the swing. My key is to concentrate on completing my backswing because, if I don't do that, my swing gets out of sync coming down.

Nowadays, the modern trend, led by Tiger Woods and others, is to curtail the length of the backswing a little. In contrast, at the top of my backswing, I like my club to be parallel to the ground, or even a little past parallel. However, irrespective of whether you have a long or a short backswing, you must ensure that at the top of the swing the bulk of your weight is on the inside of your right foot. We all have to guard against the dreaded reverse-pivot, a common fault caused by too much of your weight being kept on your left side, as this will seriously affect your generation of power.

EIGHT KEYS TO A GREAT BACKSWING

1 My left shoulder has turned under my chin. If you can't do this, check your address position. It might be because your chin is too much on your chest.

2 The left arm is straight but not tense.

3 I have allowed my left foot to come off the ground a fraction, facilitating a full shoulder turn.

4 My weight has shifted so that the bulk of it is on the inside of my right foot at the top of the backswing.

5 The right knee is still flexed, in the same position it was at address.

6 My spine angle is the same as it was at address

7 I feel as if I have swung my left arm across my chest during the backswing.

8 My right elbow is pointing to the ground.

STARTING DOWN

I start my downswing with a smooth, lateral movement of my hips, a movement that shifts my weight onto my left side. The left knee and hip rotate to the left, dragging my hands and arms down towards the ball (see above left).

In all good downswings the gap between the hands and the right shoulder increases as the club head approaches the ball. In contrast, the spine angle remains the same until well after the back is struck.

As I approach impact, note how my weight has moved further onto my left foot. My left hip is also clearing, or shifting left, enabling me to drive through the ball (above right).

APPROACHING THE MOMENT OF TRUTH

The impact position is a reflection of what has gone before. Get your grip, set up, backswing and downswing right and you will find yourself in a powerful position as your club head makes contact with the ball. Get something wrong, however, and it will show up at this point.

As we look at this photograph, taken at speed, we can see that as I approach impact I am in an extremely powerful position. My lower body is driving leftwards but my wrists are still cocked, ready to deliver the club face squarely to the ball at maximum speed. A split second later, at impact, my left arm and the club shaft will form a virtual straight line, the back of my left wrist pointing at the target.

You will also see that approaching impact my feet are still planted firmly on the ground. All too often at pro-ams I see amateurs hitting the ball off their toes, often losing their footing as a result.

SWINGING THROUGH THE BALL

THE FOLLOW THROUGH

On the backswing I felt that my left arm was swinging across my chest. In contrast, on the throughswing the hips clear and my right arm swings across my chest in what is almost a mirror-image of the backswing.

One key to solid ball striking is to swing through, not at, the ball. If you are prone to hit at it, the chances are you decelerate through impact, costing you both distance and accuracy.

At impact, about 75 per cent of my weight will be on my front foot and this increases as I drive through the ball. However, my spine angle still has not altered, even though the ball has long since been dispatched towards its target.

FINISHING OFF

For many years now, I have had four key swing thoughts that I return to whenever my game is a little off. The first is to swing back 'low and slow'. The second is to complete my backswing. The third is to initiate the downswing with a lateral movement of the hips. And the fourth is to swing to a full, balanced finished.

I cannot help but feel that many amateurs would benefit from practising a full finish, the club head ending up behind your neck, the right foot finishing as shown (see right). Of course, you cannot fake a good finish. If you lose your balance, or decelerate through impact, for example, you will struggle to complete your follow through. However, rehearsing the position while practising might well help to get you there.

PUTTING IT ALL TOGETHER

Once I have addressed the ball I start my swing slowly and smoothly with a one-piece movement of my shoulders, arms and hands. An important key for me is to take the club back low and slow. There is no need to hurry this movement. You do not hit the ball on your backswing. It is all about getting yourself into a good position to hit down and through the ball.

At the top of the backswing my shoulders have turned 90 degrees but my hips have turned only 45 degrees (opposite page). You want to feel as if you are coiled like a spring. I start my downswing with a smooth lateral movement of my hips. At impact my club and left arm are in a virtual straight line (above). The logo on my glove is pointing directly at the target.

This is the only time in the golf swing when you should feel as if your arms are fully extended (above left). My right arm has extended straight down the line and my right forearm has rolled over the left. During the follow through you should feel as if your right arm is swinging across your chest (above right). I cannot emphasise enough the importance of a full and balanced finish (right). If you can get into this position naturally, it is a sign that you are swinging well.

It would be fair to say that all golfers hit bad shots from time to time. None of us can avoid this, but, fortunately, we can do something about it if we understand what has gone wrong. The aim of this chapter is to give a step-by-step guide to curing most, if not all, of the bad shots in golf. But first we need to explain the causes of poor shots.

Curing Common Faults

In golf, most bad shots are the result of a faulty grip, poor alignment, poor swing path, or a combination of all three. When someone has a problem in all three areas, the results can be disastrous, as many amateurs know to their cost. When there is a fault in only one of these areas, the effect is less marked, but the problem still has to be ironed out if you want to play consistently good golf.

The secret is to study your ball's flight and then take the necessary steps to solve the problem. If, for example, you slice the ball, there are a number of things that you can try to cure the problem. The likelihood is that the solution is quite simple, if you know where to look for it.

HOW TO CURE THE DREADED SLICE

Most readers will not be surprised to learn that the slice is the most common fault in golf. Although 75 to 80 per cent of amateur golfers habitually slice their shots, few of them will know why they do it.

A slice is a shot that starts to the left of the target and then bends sharply to the right. This left-to-right spin on the ball is normally caused by a combination of an open club face at impact and an out-to-in swing path. The end result is that the golfer will lose accuracy *and* distance.

There are a number of reasons why a golfer slices the ball, but one of the most common is that he stands with his feet, hips and shoulders all 'open', or left of the target (see left). This is often aggravated by a weak grip (see insert), in which both the hands are turned too far left on the grip, and by an open club face at address.

When I am asked to cure someone's slice, first I ask him how he lines up his club head. This might seem like a pretty basic skill, but many golfers have no idea how to do it. The correct way to line up the club (whether it be a wood or an iron) is to ensure that the bottom edge is lined up so that it is square (or at 90 degrees) to the target. Whatever you do, you must not line up your shots with the top edge of the club, something I have seen done on a number of occasions, as this will lead to very inaccurate shots.

The next stage is to check the grip. If you are slicing, the chances are your grip is too weak, meaning you will have to move both your hands in a clockwise direction on the grip. In the last chapter, I emphasised just how vital it is to build a sound grip, one that brings the club head back square to the target at impact. And I stress that again here: without a sound grip, you will never fulfil your potential.

Once I have got the golfer's hands in the correct position, I will check his alignment, knowing full well that all slicers set up so they are pointing well to the left of the target. Sometimes, the golfer in question will not believe me when I tell him how far to the left he is aiming. In those cases, I normally put a club down at his feet and ask him to move back to beside me to see what I mean.

The slice, as I said, tends to be caused by a combination of all these factors. It can be a very destructive shot, but it can also be easily cured, provided you know how to go about it.

COMMON CAUSES OF A SLICE

• **Too weak a grip.** Both your hands are turned too far to the left on the grip. In a particularly bad case, you will see three or four knuckles on your right hand, but only one, or one and a half, on the left hand. This is a classic, all-too-common slicer's grip.

Solution – Turn your hands to the right until you can see two or three knuckles on each hand.

• **The club face is open at address.**

Solution – Make sure it is square. It amazes me how little care some golfers take when lining up the club head. But it is vital if you are to hit the ball consistently at the target. I recommend you should line up the club face first and then move your body into place, not the other way round. Remember, too, that it is the bottom edge of the club you should be lining up, not the top, as some golfers seem to think.

• **Lining up open, or left of the target, producing an outside-to-in swing.**

Solution – When you address the ball, make sure your feet, hips and shoulders are all square to the target line, or, in other words, pointing straight at the target.

• **The ball is too far forward in the stance.**

Solution – Move it back a bit. When the ball is too far forward in the stance, it forces you into an open position, increasing the chances of you swinging outside-to-in, thereby imparting slice spin on the ball.

• **Casting from the top.** Sometimes, in an effort to get back at the ball, your right shoulder becomes overactive, moving outwards and accentuating your outside-to-in swing path.

Solution – Relax. Try to think about rhythm rather than power. With your practice swing, concentrate on dropping your club head inside the line at the start of the downswing and imagine it tracking from inside as it approaches the ball.

COMMON CAUSES OF A HOOK

• **Too strong a grip.** If you hook the ball, the chances are your hands are too far to the right on the grip. If this is the case, you will see about three, maybe even four, knuckles on your left hand, but only one on your right.

Solution – Turn both hands to the left. In a good, neutral grip you should see the same number of knuckles on both hands. Normally, that will be two or three.

• **The club face is closed at address.**

Solution – Make sure the club face is square. This is crucial.

• **Lining up closed, or right of the target, encouraging an inside-to-out swing path.**

Solution – Take care to ensure that you are lined up square to the target.

• **The ball is positioned too far back in the stance.**

Solution – Move it a little forward. When the ball is too far back in your stance, it encourages you to adopt a closed address position, increasing the likelihood that you will swing inside-to-out.

• **You take the club back too quickly and too far inside the line.**

Solution – Concentrate on making a one-piece takeaway in which you move the club back in a straight line. Think about moving the butt of the club, rather than the club head, first in the takeaway. This should help you to keep the shaft of the club on line longer in the backswing and will also stop the club from becoming trapped behind you on the downswing.

GET RID OF YOUR HOOK FOR EVER

A hook is a shot that starts to the right of the target, then bends sharply to the left. It is not as common as a slice, but it is still quite prevalent, particularly among middle-to-low-handicap golfers.

The hook is normally caused by the combination of a closed club face at impact and an inside-to-out swing. Like the slice, and all other bad shots for that matter, the origin of the hook can almost always be traced to a golfer's address position. Given that this is the case, when trying to rid yourself of a hook, first check your grip and address position. As often as not, if you are hooking the ball, your grip will be too strong (see below) and you will be standing 'closed', or to the right, of the target (opposite page). Check to see if your grip and stance are causing the problem. If you are not sure, ask your PGA pro to have a look at your swing. The chances are that he will spot the problem in an instant.

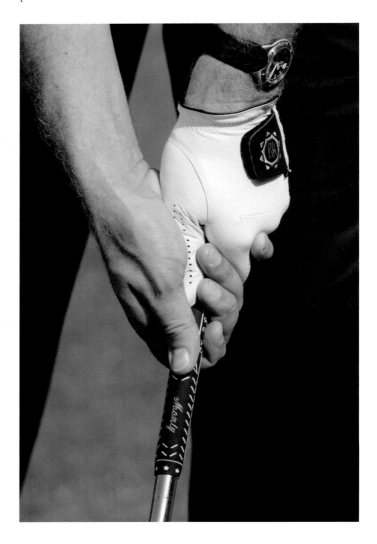

PREVENTING A PUSH

A golfer is said to have pushed a shot when he hits it in a straight line to the right of the target. Often, when you push a shot, you will feel that you have struck the ball solidly, but that is little consolation if your ball ends up in a water hazard or deep in the trees.

A push is a by-product of the same inside-to-out swing that creates a hook, but this time the club face is square, not closed, to the line of the swing. There are a number of reasons why golfers push the ball, and most, if not all, of them can be traced back to the address position.

Sometimes, although not too often, it is caused simply by addressing the ball with your club face open, pointing right of the target. When this is the case, follow the same guidelines I set out when talking about curing a slice and that should solve the problem. More commonly, the push can be caused by poor alignment. You might be standing with your feet, hips and knees all pointing to the target, but, if your shoulders are aiming right, you will push the ball. If you are prone to doing this, a good tip to help you overcome it is to address the ball holding your club in the right hand. Only after lining up your feet and hips should you bring your left hand onto the club, thereby making it easier to ensure your right shoulder is not pointing too far right. (Incidentally, if you tend to line up with your shoulders pointing left of the target, a good idea is to approach the ball holding your club in your left hand. Only after aligning your feet and hips should you place your right hand on the grip.)

Another cause of a push is dropping your club too far inside the line at the start of the downswing (see left). This means that the club gets so far behind you that you can't get it past your body. In this scenario, you are bound to push the shot, unless, of course, you realise what's happening and turn your hands over in an attempt to counteract it. When this happens, you will hit a smothered hook instead. Because it happens so quickly, this is one fault that is quite difficult to eradicate. If you do tend to get too far inside the line on the downswing, I suggest you should concentrate on clearing your hips at the start of the downswing, rather than sliding them towards the target. You might also try to concentrate on keeping your hands in front of your body, albeit making sure that this does not compromise your shoulder turn.

COMMON CAUSES OF A PUSH

• **The club face is open at address.** You might have lined up with your feet, hips and shoulders all square, or parallel, to the target but, if your club face is open, the ball is bound to fly straight right.

Solution – Take great care to line the bottom edge of your club square to the target.

• **The golfer is lined up with his club face, feet, hips and shoulders pointing to the right of the target.** In other words, the problem is not a swing fault, but poor alignment.

Solution – Make sure your feet, hips and shoulders are all square to the target.

• **Dropping the club too far inside the line at the top of the backswing.**

Solution – Concentrate on clearing your hips on the downswing rather than sliding them towards the target.

• **Moving ahead of the ball at impact.**

Solution – Concentrate on keeping your head behind the ball on the downswing.

GETTING RID OF A PULL

A pull is often caused by the opposite faults that make you push a ball. When it happens, the ball travels in a straight line to the left of the target. Like a push, it often feels solid but can be very destructive.

A pull is a by-product of the same outside-to-inside swing that causes a slice. The difference is that the club face is square, not open, to the line of swing. If you are trying to eradicate a persistent pull, first check your club face at address. Is it closed? If so, that may be the cause.

You should also check your alignment. Where, exactly, is the ball positioned in relationto your feet? If it is too far forward, it could, in turn, force your right shoulder forward, encouraging the club face to close before you make contact with the ball.

Finally, when swinging, make sure you are not leaving too much of your weight on your rear foot during the downswing (left), as this can also cause you to pull the ball.

COMMON CAUSES OF A PULL

• **The club face is closed at address.** Even if your feet, hips and shoulders are square to the target line, the ball is bound to fly left if you address the ball with your club face pointing left of the target.

Solution – Take great care to ensure your club face is square at address.

• **Club face, feet, hips and shoulders are all pointing left of the target at set-up.**

Solution – Take more care when you are addressing the ball.

• **Too much weight on your back foot.**

Solution – Concentrate on sliding your weight onto your left side at the start of the downswing.

SHAKING OFF A SHANK

There is no doubt that the shank is the most frightening shot in golf, so much so that some golfers refuse to mention it, referring to it as 'that "S" word'.

Invariably, you shank the ball when you least expect to. You might go literally months on end without shanking, and then, suddenly, you will hit one, often when things are going well. We have all experienced it, I'm afraid. You hit one good shot after another, you are starting to believe it might be your day, when, out of the blue, you hit a shank.

A shank is best described as a shot that squirts low and straight right, sometimes more than 45 degrees away from the target line. It occurs when the ball strikes the hosel of the club, rather than the face, usually, but not always, as a result of the club coming from outside the target line.

I have one friend who swears he shanks the ball only when he rolls the club face open at the start of the backswing. By doing that (see right), there is almost no way he can get the club head back to the ball. He is almost certain to hit the ball with the hosel, with disastrous results.

The problem with shanking is that once you hit one, you are likely to hit another soon after, because you will be tight and tense, making it difficult to release the club head freely. So if you do hit a shank on the golf course, try not to panic. However, if you are very worried about hitting another, why not try setting up with the ball aligned more towards the toe of the club than normal? This is not a cast-iron cure, but it might do the trick.

COMMON CAUSES OF A SHANK

• **Rolling the face of the club open at the start of the backswing.**
This creates a very flat swing plane and makes it almost impossible to bring the club face back square to the ball.

Solution – Make sure you do not fan the club open on the backswing. A good way to do this is to concentrate on keeping the grooves of your club square to the target for the first six to nine inches of the swing.

• **Hands are further away from the ball at impact than they were at address.**

Solution – Address the ball nearer the toe of the club than normal.

• **Extreme out-to-in swing path.**

Solution – Close your stance a little and then concentrate on hitting the inside of the ball.

SIX COMMON CAUSES OF LOSS OF POWER AND ACCURACY.

1 TIGHT IS NOT RIGHT

I have lost count of the number of times I have seen amateurs ruin their chances of hitting a good shot simply because they are too tense at address. This can manifest itself in a number of ways: through too much grip pressure, rigid arms, tight shoulders and so on, all of which are harmful because they reduce mobility and impair your ability to generate club-head speed.

When addressing the ball, you should feel relaxed, ready to swing the club back and through. The last thing you need is to feel that your muscles are 'grid-locked'. Jack Nicklaus once said that you should grip the club as you would an injured bird. Put another way, the secret is to grip 'light not tight' and let your arms hang freely from your shoulders.

When taking up your address position, another thing to remember is to keep your chin up, well away from your chest. Unfortunately, a lot of amateurs address the ball with their chins planted firmly on their chests (see right), making it all but impossible to turn the left shoulder under the chin during the backswing. This in turn will restrict your turn on the backswing, causing a dramatic loss of power.

2 REMEMBER TO STRIVE FOR WIDTH

Another common mistake amateurs make is to pick up the club on the backswing (see right), something that starts a chain reaction that leads to loss of width, a steep downswing, deep divots and a choppy attack at the ball.

At the start of the backswing the club, hands, arms and shoulders should move away from the ball as a unit. You should endeavour to take the club back 'low and slow' in a one-piece movement. Once you have learned to do that, you will not only accumulate power, but establish a rhythm that can be maintained throughout the swing.

3 MAKE THE MOST OF YOUR TURN

In golf, the whole purpose of the backswing is to wind yourself up like a spring, something that can be achieved only if you learn to maximise your shoulder turn, while at the same time keeping your hip turn to a minimum.

Convention dictates that in an ideal backswing the shoulders should turn through 90 degrees, while the hips turn through 45 degrees. However, few amateur golfers ever achieve this. Instead, some turn both their hips and shoulders 90 degrees, while others turn very little, swinging with their hands and arms instead. Either way, little power is generated (see left).

To build a powerful backswing, you have to learn to maximise your shoulder turn, while at the same time using your right knee to restrict your hip turn. During the backswing, your right knee should remain flexed throughout, acting as an anchor to cut down hip movement. To achieve this, it helps if you keep your weight on the inside of your right foot during the backswing. It helps, too, to feel as if you are sitting on your right hip. Whatever you do, you must not allow your right knee to straighten as this will mean all resistance is lost. Then, you might well achieve a big turn, but will not create an effective coil.

4 CASTING AWAY YOUR POWER

Casting the club at the top of the backswing is a common problem among amateur golfers, and it is one that can lead to a considerable loss of power.

By 'casting the club', I mean uncocking the wrists, or releasing the club, too early during the downswing (see above), resulting in the golfer flicking weakly at the ball. As far as I am concerned, the downswing should always be initiated, not by the hands and arms but by a lateral movement of the hips towards the target. That is one of my swing keys: a hip movement starts it and the hands and arms are dragged down as a result.

5 AVOID ALL UNNECESSARY MOVEMENT

By its very nature, the golf swing is a complicated manoeuvre, but that should not stop you striving to make your swing as simple and repeatable as possible.

What you need is a good turn on your backswing and a good turn on your downswing. What you must avoid at all costs is horizontal movement. I wish I had a pound for every amateur I have seen who moved his head up on the backswing and then down on the downswing. Sometimes, of course, he

gets away with it, but not consistently, particularly when his timing is off.

To simplify the movement, it is vitally important to keep your head as steady as possible throughout the swing. You should not feel as if your head is locked into position, as this would create unwanted tension, but all horizontal movement up and down should be eliminated, as this is the prime cause of thin and fat shots.

Concentrating on keeping your right knee flexed during the backswing is one good way to keep horizontal movement to a minimum. Another is to think about

keeping your spine angle constant throughout the swing. For those who have not thought much about spine angle, let me explain. Look at the photograph above and you will see that at address I have bent at the hips so that my spine angle is about 35 or 40 degrees off vertical. Now glance at the other photographs and you will see that I have retained this angle not only at the top of the backswing, and through impact, but until well after the ball is struck. That is what is meant by retaining your spine angle during the swing, and it is a vital factor in playing consistently good golf.

6 LEARN TO SWING, NOT HIT

I would be willing to bet that no matter how many instruction books you have read, you will never have found any reference to a golf 'hit', as opposed to a golf 'swing'. That is because successive generations of teachers have found that it is much more efficient to 'swing through' the ball rather than 'hit at it'.

Unfortunately, however, that is a message that has not got through to a lot of amateur golfers. They take a long backswing and then hit down at the ball, invariably with disastrous results.

If you are guilty of this, why not concentrate on trying to 'pose' at the top of your follow through? Imagine you are Tiger Woods, for example, and swing through to a full finish like he does. Put another way, concentrate on getting your belt buckle to point at, or even to the left of, the target at the end of your swing, and then hold that position for a second or two as if you are posing for the cameras.

Strange though it may sound, if you concentrate on 'posing', or holding, your follow through, it will also benefit your balance. Often, amateurs lose their balance because they are concentrating so hard on hitting the ball that it becomes a source of tension. The good news is that you can practise a fluid movement by swishing at a dandelion or a twig. While doing this, feel as if you swing through, rather than to, the object and then try to replicate that feeling when it comes to hitting the ball.

In golf, unlike most other sports, the terrain you play on constantly changes. During the course of a round of golf, you will find yourself in many different positions and will sometimes need to alter your stance, even your swing, to play the necessary shot.

Speciality Shots

What follows is a simple guide to how to play most, if not all, of the shots you will require during a normal round of golf. Learn them and you will be able to cope with almost every eventuality.

Remember, to score really well, you must be able to shape your shots in both directions as and when required. Some good players struggle to hit a hook or a slice but the great ones can bend the ball at will.

HOW TO HIT A FADE

Readers who have watched me in action will know that the fade is my stock shot. It is the shot I feel most comfortable with and the one I will hit unless the situation requires something else.

My normal set-up enables me to hit a fade at will, but if you are trying to manufacture a left-to-right shot you might have to make a few adjustments to do it.

First you have to set up so that your club head is aiming directly at the target (see opposite page). Next, alter your stance so that your feet, hips and shoulders are all aiming to the left (see opposite page). The key thing to remember is that your feet,

hips and shoulders are parallel to where you want the ball to start, and the club head is square to where you want the ball to finish.

From this position, all you have to do is swing the club along the line of your set-up, allowing the combination of the out-to-in set-up and the square club face to impart fade spin on the ball. It is worth bearing in mind that the further left you aim, the more your ball will fade. But remember, a fade tends to fly less far than a draw so, if you are attempting to hit a big slice, you will need to take more club than you would normally use.

Once you have got yourself into the correct address position for the shot you want to hit, swing the club along the line of your set-up, allowing the combination of the out-to-in set-up and the square club face to impart spin on the ball.

In the past, some teachers have advocated that you should weaken your grip to hit a fade (and strengthen it to hit a draw), but I do not think that is necessary. However, you might find holding your club a little more firmly with the left hand through impact will help you to produce the left-to-right flight you want.

If you get your set-up right, it will not be long before you can 'move' the ball left-to-right. Once you have mastered that, the next step is to learn how to control that movement in the air. The only way to do it, I'm afraid, is through experimenting with your stance. Start with it, say, 20 degrees open, and you will see that the ball fades only five to ten yards through the air. However, stand 30 degrees open and you will notice that you can generate a bigger fade. Once you get the feel for it, practise hitting different fades. You will soon learn how you need to set up in order to shape the shot the amount you want.

HOW TO HIT A DRAW

When you want to hit a draw, the principles are the same as for the fade. The secret, as with the fade, is to set up correctly and then commit to the shot.

For the draw, you need to set up so that your feet, hips and shoulders are all aiming to the right and the club head is square to the target (opposite page). As with the fade, the club head points to where you want the ball to finish, the feet, hips and shoulders aim at where you want the ball to start.

Once you are set up correctly, swing down the line you have created, allowing the combination of an in-to-out swing path and a square club head to create the draw spin you want.

If you want to draw a drive, tee the ball nice and high. Conversely, it is easier to fade a ball if you tee it up low.

PLAYING FROM AN UPHILL LIE

When faced with an uphill lie, you will need to hit more club than normal. If it is a steep hill, you might need two more clubs than usual. On a more gentle slope one extra club might well do.

On slopes, you also have to adapt your set-up to suit. When playing off a flat lie, your shoulders will automatically be almost parallel to the ground, but on a slope you have to alter your set-up to achieve this. To get your shoulders parallel to the slope, ensure there is more weight on your back foot than normal. Exactly how much is dependent on the severity of the slope.

In this position your leg movement and weight transference will be somewhat restricted. Almost invariably, your hands will take over, causing the club head to close through impact and a hook to ensue. To counteract this, aim to the right of the target.

In the photos you will see that my ball is a little further back in my stance than normal. This is because, when playing on an upslope, you can easily get stuck on your back foot. Moving your ball back in your stance enables you to counteract this and make good contact with the ball.

PLAYING FROM
A DOWNHILL LIE

With a downhill lie, you will also have
to adapt your set-up and alignment to
counteract the slope. As with the uphill
lie, you need to address the ball with the
bulk of your weight on your lower foot,
thereby ensuring your shoulders are
parallel to the slope. In contrast to an
uphill lie, the tendency is to slice the ball
off a downhill lie, so you should aim
left, not right, of the target.

For this shot, I have the ball in the
centre of my stance at address,
encouraging the club head to follow
the contour of the slope. I also keep my
knees flexed throughout the swing,
ensuring that I stay down all the way
through the ball.

In this situation you tend to hit the
ball a little further than you would from
a flat lie. So, if you are faced with what
would normally be a 5-iron shot, hit a
6-iron instead.

PLAYING A BALL ABOVE YOUR FEET

When your ball is above your feet, your swing plane will automatically flatten, which in turn will lead to the ball hooking a little. The secret is to work out how much the ball will move from right to left in the air and then take your stance to counteract that movement.

You will see from the main photo that my ball is about 4 to 5 inches above my feet. For this shot, I need to aim my feet, hips and shoulders about 10 yards to the right of the target. If the slope had been more severe, I would aim further to the right. Conversely, if it had been more gentle, I would aim less to the right.

When I take my stance, I feel as if my weight is leaning into the slope a little. I have also deliberately gripped down the shaft so that the ball is closer to my hands. From here I will swing back a little flatter than normal. The tendency is also to swing round too much on the downswing, which would cause too much of a draw. To counteract this, I concentrate on finishing high with my hands above my shoulders.

PLAYING A BALL BELOW YOUR FEET

In this scenario, I know the slope will cause the ball to fade in the air so I make sure that I take aim with my feet, hips and shoulders well to the left of the target.

You should grip at the top of the club, ensuring that you flex your knees a little more than usual. You should also keep your weight back on your heels more than normal, ensuring you maintain your balance throughout the swing.

Given the slope, your backswing will be a little more upright than is normally the case. This does not matter. But beware: when hitting this sort of shot it is easy to come over the top at the start of the downswing, so concentrate on coming down inside the line.

PLAYING INTO THE WIND

When faced with a shot into the wind, the first thing to do is gauge how much of an effect it will have on your ball. Is it a one-club wind? Is it a two-club wind? In my experience, amateurs tend to under-club rather than over-club and then try to force the shot. That is the worst thing you can do, because, by hitting the ball hard, you will hit it higher, exposing it to the worst of the elements.

Once you have chosen your club, adapt your stance to suit the conditions. When playing into the wind, you should be trying to keep the ball low, under the elements, so move your ball a little further back in your stance than normal (see top right). You don't want to be blown about in the wind so you should also widen your stance and crouch over the ball for a fraction more than usual.

Taking the club back low and slow is something I always concentrate on, but it is even more important when hitting into the wind. The last thing you want to do is pick up the club and then drop it back down on the ball as this will result in a high shot. Instead, concentrate on keeping your backswing nice and wide (see middle right) and then stay down a little longer through impact (see far right). Above all, do not force the shot. Give yourself plenty of club and then swing slowly and smoothly, letting the club do the work for you.

PLAYING DOWNWIND

When I am playing downwind, I set up much the same way as I would in calm conditions. The only concession I make is to move the ball a touch forward in my stance (right), encouraging me to hit it a little on the upswing to create a higher flight.

When swinging, you should concentrate on keeping your balance but, at the same time, you might also try to hit the ball harder than normal as this will get the ball in the air, taking full advantage of the conditions. But be careful not to hit at the ball. Instead, swing through it, to a full and balanced finish (far right).

PLAYING IN A CROSSWIND

In a crosswind first alter your aim in order to allow for the wind. For example, if there is a 10 m.p.h. wind coming from your right, you should aim about ten yards to the right, knowing the wind will move your ball back towards the target. If the wind is stronger, say 20 m.p.h., you will need to aim further right, maybe twenty yards, because the ball will move more in the air.

When deciding where to aim, it is important to take your normal shape of shot into consideration. If, for example, you hit the ball right-to-left and are faced with a wind from the right, you will need to aim further right than someone who hits the ball left-to-right. Likewise, if you are a fader, and are faced with a shot with wind from the left, you will need to aim further left than someone who hits the ball right-to-left. Your normal shape of shot might also impact on your club selection. If, for example, you are a fader, playing in a right-to-left wind, you might need to use an extra club because, effectively, what you are doing is playing more into the wind than someone who draws the ball. However, someone who draws his shots, when playing in a right-to-left wind, should take less club than normal because the shape of his shot means his ball will be riding the wind and will run when it lands.

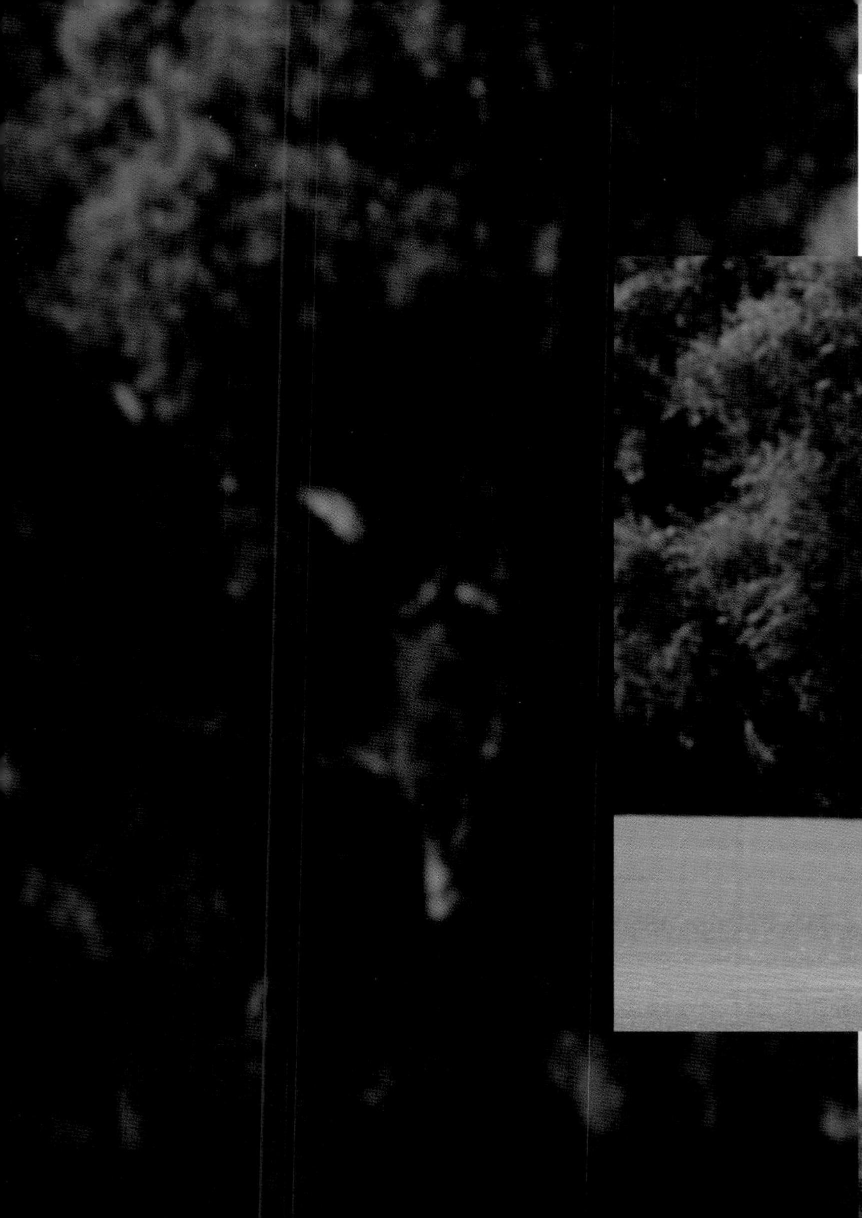

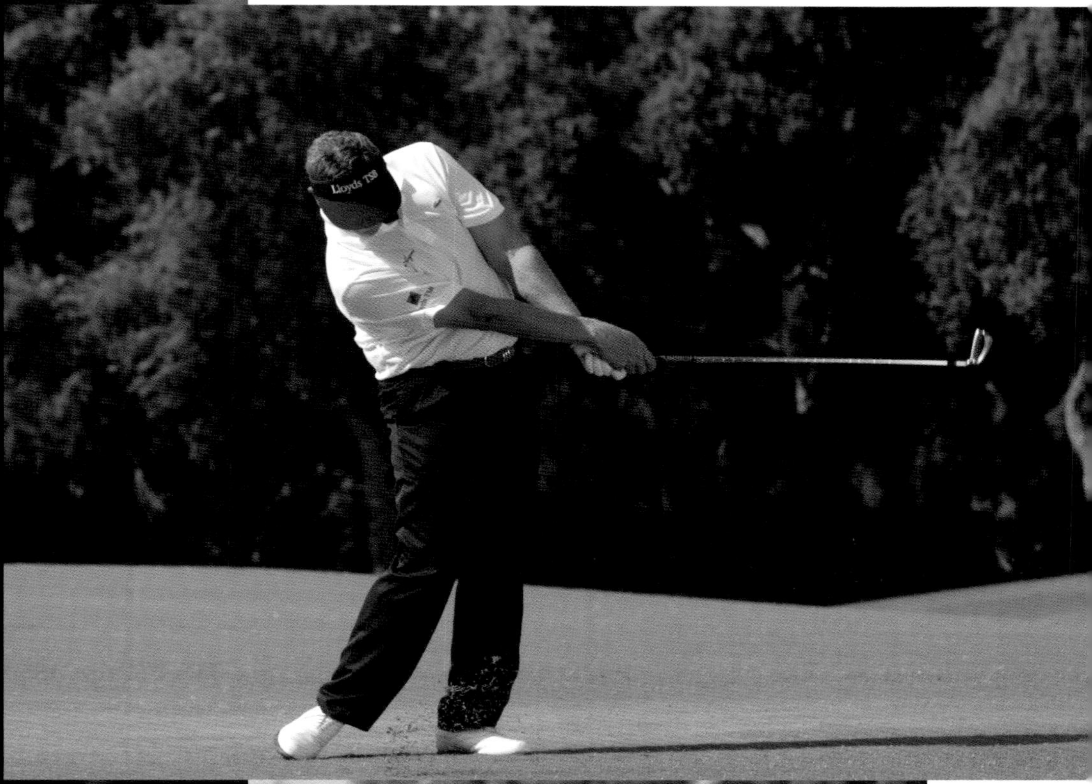
Lloyds TSB

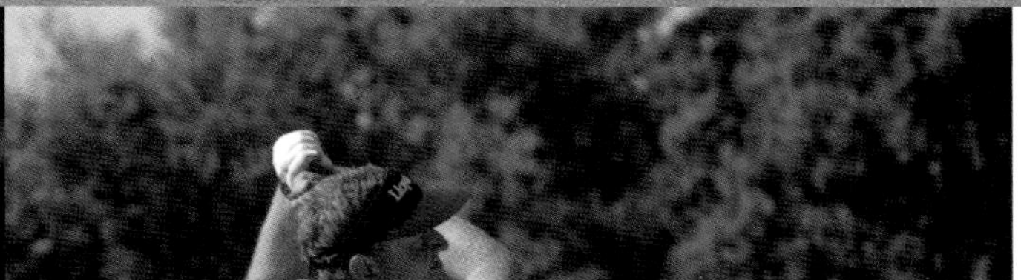

HOW TO HIT A PUNCH SHOT

When playing into a wind, a punch shot can be highly effective, boring through the wind and then stopping abruptly when landing. Certainly, it is a shot that's well worth learning, especially if you play a lot of links golf.

As with most shots, the set-up is vital. When hitting a punch, you need to set up with your club well back in your stance, not far from the inside of the right foot (see left). This means that the hands will be further ahead of the ball than normal, which delofts the club and creates the downward blow required.

At address, I start with about 70 per cent of my weight on my left foot, where it remains for most of the swing. From there, I concentrate on making a short backswing (above left) and then driving down and through to an abbreviated finish (above).

The secret to this shot is to be aggressive. Feel as if you are punching down at the back of the ball, driving it low towards the target. Try it with a wedge initially, then experiment with your other clubs. Keep practising and you will soon get a feel for the distance you hit each club.

HOW TO HIT A SHOT FROM A BARE LIE

Many golfers, particularly those used to playing on lush inland courses, panic whenever they are faced with a shot from a bare lie. However, such shots should not be frightening, provided you know how to deal with them.

The secret to this shot is to hit the ball first and then the turf. When faced with a ball on a bare, scruffy lie, some golfers tend to look up too quickly, causing them to thin the shot. Others do the opposite and dig at the ball, resulting in them hitting the shot fat. In both instances the bad shots are caused by too much horizontal body movement, or, put another way, loss of spine angle during the swing.

When playing a shot from a bare lie, address the ball with your hands a little further forward than normal, and with the ball well back in your stance (above). Then swing back, down and through, being careful to concentrate on maintaining your spine angle until well after impact (right).

HOW TO PLAY A SHOT OUT OF A DIVOT

Golf can sometimes be a cruel game, never more so than when you hit a drive straight down the middle, only to find your ball has come to rest in a divot.

When you find yourself in a divot, take your address with your hands slightly further forward than normal. Grip down the club a little and play the ball well back in your stance.

It is very important to hit the ball first and the ground second when faced with this shot. It is also vital to hit down and through the ball, not at it. You should be thinking about extending the divot as you swing through the ball. That will ensure a solid contact and give you the best chance of escaping with your good score intact.

HOW TO PLAY A LEFT-HANDED SHOT

Tiger Woods had a problem on his hands when he hit his drive into the trees on the third hole during the final round of the 2003 Masters at Augusta National. He found he could not take his normal stance because a bush was in his way, so all he could do was reverse his club head and attempt to hit it out left-handed.

The first step is to address the ball like a lefty, either with the toe of the club head pointing towards the ground (see right) or with the back of the club head facing the ball. It makes sense to use your wedge or a sand wedge for this shot, because they have bigger heads than your other clubs and will therefore give you more of a chance of making good contact with the ball.

When I am playing this shot I concentrate on keeping my body as quiet as possible. The objective is not to hit the ball a long way, but rather to get the ball out of trouble by the easiest route. You should try to hit the ball with a descending blow, so address it with about 60 per cent of your weight on your front foot and with the ball positioned well back in your stance. Then concentrate on swinging your arms back and through, keeping the rest of your body as still as possible. Keep the distance you hit the ball as short as possible in order to get out of trouble as this will minimise mistakes.

An alternative way to play this shot can be seen at the bottom of the opposite page. In this instance, I have addressed the ball facing directly away from it and have then swung my right arm straight back and through. Some people find this easier than the left-handed escape shot; others do not. Personally, I find it rather difficult, but, if you do try to use it, remember to keep your body as still as possible. Any body movement could mean you miss the ball altogether.

PART 2

THE
SHORT
GAME

I think it was Willie Park, the first Open champion, who once said that 'a man who can putt is a match for anyone', and he was quite right, of course. No matter what level you play at, the success of a round will almost always depend largely on how you putted, so it is essential you spend much of your practice time working on this aspect of your game.

How to Putt Well
All the Time

The good news, however, is that you do not have to be naturally athletic to be a good putter. Unlike hitting a driver 300 yards straight down the middle, it does not require physical prowess. Anyone can achieve success, provided, that is, that he or she is blessed with touch and feel and has a basic understanding of the mechanics. However, to be a good putter you do need to develop a method that repeats. For a nine-foot putt, the margin for error is much smaller than it would be for a 250-yard 3-wood shot. The hole is only $4\frac{1}{4}$ inches (108mm) in diameter, which is not much when you consider you have the stroke, the line, the speed and the green conditions to think about.

Within this chapter, I hope to teach you sound mechanics, and much else besides, but first a word of warning. There is no such thing as one, and only one, way to putt. Even great golfers have changed their style. When it comes down to it, we all have to experiment to find what works best for us. As a general rule, I would suggest that if you putt well already, you should stick with what you have got, irrespective of how you do it. However, if your putting is inconsistent, and you miss more putts than you should, it is time to review your method. That is what I did during 2002 and it produced almost instantaneous results.

HOW I USE THE BELLY PUTTER

ADDRESS

One of the great things about using a belly putter is that you do not have to learn a new grip, as you would if you decided to switch from a short putter to a broomhandle putter, as used by Sam Torrance and Bernhard Langer, among others. I grip the belly putter with a cack-handed grip, with my right hand below my left. That is a personal preference, others will choose to use a more conventional grip.

THE BACKSWING

Having the butt of the putter wedged into your midriff helps you create a pure pendulum movement. As long as the putter does not become dislodged, there can be no independent movement of the hands and arms, thereby eliminating one of the most common causes of poor putting. Here, the triangle formed between my shoulders and arms remains the same as it was at address. There has been no unnecessary movement, nothing that can cause problems when you are under pressure.

THE FOLLOW THROUGH

This is the mirror image of the last shot and shows how, when used correctly, the belly putter can be extremely effective. Again, there has been breakdown in the triangle formed between the shoulders and the arms, even though the ball is already well on its way. The pendulum movement is working perfectly, leaving me to concentrate fully on the line and length of the putt.

WHY I USE A BELLY PUTTER AND HOW IT COULD WORK FOR YOU

Midway through the 2002 season my putting became so erratic that I realised I needed to take drastic action. That is when I switched to using a belly putter, and it is a move that I have only occasionally regretted since. Over the last eighteen months or so my putting has improved immeasurably and the sole reason for this is my switch to a longer putter. I am sure it could work for you, too.

There are a number of benefits that accrue from using a belly putter, but by far the most important is that it creates a pure pendulum movement. It eradicates all the independent arm and wrist movements that are the causes of most missed putts. When I look at old pictures of me using a short putter I can see what I was doing wrong. I used to take the club back a bit outside the line and then cut across it coming through. There was also a lot of independent arm movement, but that has been eliminated altogether now that I use a belly putter. The fact that the putter is wedged into my stomach means that it is almost impossible to do anything other than take the putter straight back and straight through. It also makes it extremely difficult to hinge your wrists at takeaway or for your arms to separate from your body during the follow through. Thanks to the belly putter, my putting is much more consistent than it has ever been before. It is also much more reliable under pressure, as I showed in my Ryder Cup singles match against Scott Hoch when I seemed to hole almost everything I stood up to.

The belly putter has one other big advantage: it is easy to use. It does not require you to make massive modifications to your current putting technique. You take your normal grip. You assume your normal address position. You can even get a PGA professional to extend your existing putter if you want to. The sole thing that is different is that it is anchored into your mid-section, and that is what makes it so effective.

USING THE BELLY PUTTER – THE VIEW FROM THE OTHER SIDE

ADDRESS

My address position is very similar to how it used to be when I used a shorter putter. My feet are a little open. My arms hang from my shoulders. The only difference is that the end of the putter is wedged into my stomach. It is worth pointing out that ball position is vital when using a belly putter. You should be endeavouring to make contact when the putter head is just past the lowest point of its arc. You will probably have to experiment a little until you find that point.

THE BACKSWING

The first thing you notice when you use a belly putter is how solid the stroke feels. There is no independent movement of the hands and arms. There should be little or no body movement, either. Concentrate on maintaining the triangle throughout the swing and you will not go far wrong. The length of the putt determines the length of the backswing. Keep it nice and short on short putts and accelerate through the ball.

THE FOLLOW THROUGH

The belly putter helps you to create a pendulum movement. The length of the backswing should be the same as the length of the follow through. The pace of the swing should also be constant. Refrain from looking up until well after the putter has made contact with the ball. It might be a bit of a cliché, but 'listen for them dropping' is still sound advice irrespective of what type of putter you use.

HOW TO CHOOSE A BELLY PUTTER

Most belly putters are about 10 to 12 inches longer than a standard putter. They come with two grips, or with one extended grip, like mine. When buying a belly putter, it is vital to get one that is the correct length for you. Bear in mind that the grip end of the putter should be anchored about two inches above your belly button and you will not go far wrong.

MY PUTTING GRIP

You will see from the photograph (right) that I use a cack-handed grip with my belly putter. When I started to use the belly putter I gripped the club conventionally (with my right hand below the left), but I found that I got much better results when I switched them round so that my left hand is below the right. I found that using a cack-handed grip helps you to square up your shoulders at address. Try it and you will see what I mean. When I used the conventional grip, I tended to stand with my shoulders a little open, which meant that I pushed a lot of putts. The cack-handed grip solved that problem overnight.

From this close-up photograph, you will see my hands are in a neutral position, with the palm of the left hand parallel to the palm of the right hand, and with both thumbs pointing straight down the shaft. This means that the hands work together, rather than fighting against each other, helping me to keep the putter head square throughout the stroke. It is a prerequisite for good putting, irrespective of whether you putt cack-handed or not.

Just by looking at them, you can see that my hands are relaxed at the address position. When putting, your grip should be firm enough to control the putter, but not so tight as to create tension. This is important because excessive grip tension is one of the prime causes of missed putts.

THE CHOICE IS YOURS

I would thoroughly recommend all golfers to give the belly putter a go. However, being realistic, I know most golfers will not accept this advice and will continue to use a shorter putter instead. That is your call, and I am certainly not going to criticise you for it, but, if you are going stick with a conventional putter, there are some things you have to remember. Putting is very personal. There are lots of ways to hole putts, but, in my experience, the best putters are those who keep it simple. For that reason, I am a great believer in keeping the wrists out of the putting stroke as much as possible (something that happens automatically with the belly putter). So I would recommend you should putt with your arms and shoulders, keeping the triangle formed between the shoulders and the arms constant throughout the swing.

PUTTING WITH A REGULATION PUTTER

THE SET-UP

In my experience, most good putters address the ball with their feet, hips and shoulders square or slightly open to the target. Likewise, most stand with their feet roughly shoulder-width apart, with the ball positioned somewhere between the left toe and the centre of the stance, and with their eyes directly over the ball. You will have to experiment to work out what works best for you. However, I should stress that I have never seen a good putter who stands with the ball well back in his stance, as this would lead to a downward hit, making the ball jump rather than roll smoothly off the putter.

The grip is also a matter of personal choice. There are no dos and don'ts when it comes to gripping a putter. However, if you are putting poorly, I would suggest you make sure you are setting up with your hands parallel to each other, thereby helping them to work together. To do this, take your stance with your hands facing each other on either side of the grip. Then, grip the club, being careful to ensure that both thumbs are pointing straight, or almost straight, down the grip.

Talking of grips, one of the best pieces of advice I have ever received concerned grip pressure. At the time, I was holding the putter much too tightly, thereby introducing tension and cutting down feel. I was encouraged to hold the putter just firmly enough so that I did not lose control of it. Even now, when using the belly putter, 'grip light, not tight' remains one of my key thoughts.

THE BACKSWING

Once you have set up comfortably, have a last look at the target. To do this, swivel rather than lift your head. If you lift your head, you will see the line slightly differently, and doubts might be planted in your mind.

If you have played golf for a while, you have probably heard the two expressions 'take the putter straight back from the ball' and 'keep the putter head low to the ground'. Neither is wrong, although both can be misleading if, in an effort to achieve them, you overdo it and start to use your hands too much. Instead, in my opinion, you should concentrate on keeping the hands, and wrists, out of the stroke altogether. Feel as if you are putting with your shoulders and arms in what is effectively a pendulum movement, the triangle created between your shoulders and arms being maintained throughout the swing. Only on very long putts should there be any breaking of the wrists, either on the backswing or the follow through.

THE FOLLOW THROUGH

One of the most common causes of missed putts is decelerating the club through impact. Normally this happens because the backswing is either too long or too quick, forcing you to slow down in order not to hit the ball too far. To overcome this, curtail your backswing and then accelerate the putter into, and through, the ball, ensuring that the follow through is the same length, or even a little longer, than the backswing.

Good putters tend to hit their putts on the upswing, imparting top spin on the ball. This is something to work on, but be careful not to overdo this as it will lead to excessive movement and reduce the consistency of your stroke. The old adage 'listen for your putts dropping into the hole' is worth remembering, particularly on the short putts, because, if you can do this, the chances are you will have kept all unnecessary movement to a minimum.

My 100-Putt Drill

Every now and then, when I have been putting poorly, I go back to this drill, taught to me by my old coach at Houston Baptist University, Dave Mannen. It is a highly effective drill that improves not only your putting stroke but your concentration levels.

Place a ball about two feet from the hole. If you hole it, drop another in the same place and do it again. The aim is to hole 100 consecutive two-footers. If you miss, you have to start all over again.

This drill isn't really about holing the first seventy or eighty putts. They are relatively straightforward. However, as you get closer to the 100th, the pressure starts to mount. When this happens, take your time, back away, line up each putt and then concentrate on making a smooth, positive stroke.

Find a Grip that Works for You

Over the years, golfers have invented all sorts of grips designed to cure putting problems. Some, like the cack-handed grip (bottom) and the claw grip (top), have proved popular. Others have disappeared altogether.

With the cack-handed grip, the one I use, the golfer places the left hand below the right, rather than the conventional other way round. This encourages you to line up with your shoulders square to the target. It also helps to minimise wrist movement and helps you to pull the putter through impact and beyond. The disadvantage is that it is uncomfortable to start with, something that is enough to put off a lot of people.

The claw grip was first used by Chris DiMarco and has subsequently been copied and adapted by others, including former Open champion Mark Calcavecchia. As with the cack-handed grip, the left hand dominates. The right is simply placed on the grip to provide a bit of control.

HOW TO READ GREENS

world, particularly on Bermuda grass greens, it is a factor that has to be taken into account when lining up a putt. You have to remember that putts 'down' (or with) the grain will be quicker than normal, whereas putts 'against' (or into) the grain will be slower. More often than not, you should be able to tell whether a putt is down or against the grain simply by looking at the colour of the grass between your ball and the hole. When faced with a down-grain putt, the grass will appear light or shiny. In contrast, when you are putting against the grain, it will be much darker in colour. If in any doubt, look into the hole itself: you can normally see which direction the grass is growing in (see left).

Sometimes, on flattish greens, or on greens with little or no grain, you will see the right line almost immediately. However, at other times, the line will not be as obvious, so you might want to look at it not just from behind but also from the side.

Obviously, you should never hit a putt until you are ready, but try not to take too long doing it. A good idea is to study the line while your playing partner is putting, provided, of course, that you won't be getting in his way. Then, when it is your turn, you will be ready to play without too much delay.

Talking of your playing partner, if he is putting before you, it makes sense to watch him. He might not have the same putt as you, but you should still learn something by the way his ball reacts as it approaches the hole. Likewise, do not look away in disgust if you think you have missed the hole. Instead, watch the putt, because you will get a good idea of what the one coming back is likely to do.

In my experience, some people read greens better than others but, even if you are good at it, you still need to take care, especially on long, undulating putts that might break two or more different ways. When I am faced with a big-breaking putt, like the one illustrated here (see right), I pick out a spot I want the ball to pass over and then concentrate on rolling my ball over that spot at a pace that will ensure it stops around the hole.

In Britain, it is rare to find 'grain' on the greens because the grass tends to grow straight up. However, around the

START WORKING
BEFORE YOU REACH THE GREEN

Becoming a good reader of greens is vital if you want to putt well, and, as far as I am concerned, the process starts long before you reach the putting surface. I would recommend that, as you walk towards a green, you check to see how the land lies. Spending a couple of minutes looking to see if the green slopes from back to front, or right to left, could pay rich dividends, particularly on a course you do not know well. Obviously, you will not be able to see subtle breaks from this sort of distance. Nevertheless, the view I've got here does give me some precious information that might be vital as and when the time comes to select my line.

PUTTING IN THE WIND

When playing links golf, you should remember that it is
not just your long shots but also your putts that can be
affected by the wind. A strong downwind, for example, will
cause a ball to roll much further than normal. Likewise, a
crosswind can alter the line of the putt quite considerably.

   When putting in the wind, I try to gauge what sort of
effect it will have and then aim and hit the putt accordingly.
I also tend to widen my stance a little because the last thing
I want is to be blown about when I am making the stroke.
In the most inclement conditions, I will also hover my
putter head above the ground rather than ground it. The
reason for this is simple. Under the Rules of Golf, if you
ground the putter and the ball is then moved by the wind,
you are adjudged to have addressed it and will incur a
one-shot penalty. However, if you have not grounded the
putter and the ball moves, you will escape any penalty
because you are deemed not to have addressed the ball.

DISTANCE IS MORE IMPORTANT THAN LINE

When putting, it is important to remember that judgement of distance is a lot more important than getting the line right. After all, how often do you miss the hole by five or six feet to the left or right of the hole? Probably not too often, I would guess. But how often do you hit a putt five feet long or short? Rather more often, I suspect.

When I am faced with a longish putt, say of forty feet or more, I concentrate most on getting the distance right. Obviously, it would be nice to hole the putt, but, realistically, I know that doesn't happen very often. Instead, I imagine a three-foot circle around the hole and try to get my ball into that.

Often I am asked how I manage to gauge distance so accurately, but I'm afraid there is no secret answer. It's all down to practice, preferably on different types of putting surface. Once you have played golf for a while, you will find that your judgement of distance improves, but, if you want to accelerate your learning, I would suggest that you find an undulating area to practise on and then hit as many different uphill and downhill putts as possible.

Another good drill is to hit forty or fifty balls to different targets. For example, you might start by hitting five balls to a target about ten feet away. Having done that, hit five more to a target thirty feet away. Then try twenty-foot putts, forty-five-foot putts, etc. When doing this, remember not to putt at the targets in ascending or descending order of distance. Instead, select the target randomly; this will improve your feel much more quickly.

Finally, arguably the best way to improve your feel is to practise putting to a target with your eyes closed. Hit a putt and then, before opening your eyes, guess how close it is. You will be surprised how quickly your distance control improves.

BEWARE OF READING TOO MUCH BORROW

All too often, golfers fall into the trap of looking for breaks that are not there, particularly on putts of six feet or under.

When faced with a six-foot putt that you are not sure about, I suggest that you forget about break and hit it firmly straight into the middle of the hole. That way, even if it does move an inch or so, you should still hole out.

This is particularly important if you happen to be putting on slow greens, where the ball will tend to break much less than on fast putting surfaces. As a general rule, you have to allow more break on fast greens than slow greens, on short as well as long putts. One obvious example is Augusta National, the home of the Masters. Watch the tournament on TV and you will see that the competitors seldom have a straight putt, even from three feet or under.

Glance at the European Tour's Reuters Performance Statistics and you will see that even the most accurate Tour professionals hit fewer than 80 per cent of greens in regulation during a round of golf. On the other three or four holes they rely on their short games to scramble par figures.

Sharpen up Your Short Game

Tour professionals are well aware of how important it is to chip and pitch well, and it is an aspect of the game that is even more important for amateur golfers because they tend to miss many more greens than the pros. It is no exaggeration to say that the ability to chip and pitch well can mean the difference between posting a good score and a bad one.

In this chapter I will show you how to play all the shots I use when I am within sixty yards of the green. I will start with the basic pitch and the basic chip, but will go on to explain some of the specialist shots you will need when you are trying to turn three shots into two.

How to Play the Basic Pitch

This is the shot I normally use when I am between twenty and sixty yards from a green. It is what I would call a bread-and-butter shot, a shot you must master if you are to learn how to improve your scores.

You will see that when I play a pitch I have the ball positioned just to the left of the centre of my stance. That is exactly the same place from where I would hit a full wedge shot, and remains constant irrespective of the distance I want to hit the ball. You will also see that I set up with my shoulders square

to the target but with my feet a little open or left of the target line. I become more open as the shot gets shorter, up to a maximum of just under 45 degrees. I address the ball with about 60 per cent of my weight on my left foot and with my hands a fraction ahead of the ball. My grip pressure is a little more relaxed than it would be for a full shot, but not so light that I lose control.

When playing a pitch shot, your swing should feel like a truncated version of your full swing. You should start it with

your hands and arms moving together and should keep your rhythm smooth throughout.

This is a shot that you have to spend quite some time practising because distance control comes from the length of your backswing. Swing speed remains virtually constant irrespective of whether you intend to hit the shot thirty yards or sixty yards. However, for a sixty-yard shot, I will swing back to about the three-quarter position, whereas for a thirty-yard shot my backswing will be a few degrees less.

The most common mistake with this sort of shot is to swing back too far and then decelerate into the ball. There should be no attempt to hit at it or to scoop it. Instead, you should feel as if you are releasing the club freely through the ball with the through swing being about the same length as the backswing.

This is a finesse shot in which there is very little weight transference. It is all about feel and about caressing the ball towards the hole. When hit correctly, the ball should fly high and then land softly and run towards the hole.

Were you to ask them, I am sure most Tour professionals would tell you that the pitch is a fairly straightforward shot, one where 'touch' or 'feel' is just as important as technique. This is because few professionals have any difficulty with this shot, even when water, or a large bunker, lurks between their ball and the target.

However, for some amateurs, the sight of a water hazard or a deep bunker in front of them can cause such extreme anxiety that they forget the basic technique and turn into gibbering wrecks. If you are one of those, I would recommend that you try to blot out the cause of your anxiety (i.e., the water or bunker). Select a club that will enable you to clear the hazard comfortably, focus on a spot at the back of the green as your

landing area, take a lighter grip than normal, and then concentrate on swinging slowly back and accelerating through.

While on the subject of pitching, I have noticed that many amateurs tend to come up short with their pitches, especially from fifty to sixty yards out. If that is one of your faults, it could help if you concentrated on trying to land the ball on the top of the flagstick. Focus on the pin, and then try to hold that picture in your mind as you hit the shot.

Finally, make sure you keep your head down until the ball is well away. It may be a bit of an old cliché, but 'lifting your head' before contact is bound to lead to bad shots.

STAND TALL TO THE BALL

We have already seen how important good posture is in the long game, and it is just as vital when it comes to hitting a wedge into the green. The wedge might be one of the shortest clubs in your bag, but that does not mean that you have to hunch over the ball with your back rounded and your hands close to your knees. All the good wedge players I know stand tall to the ball. They bend forward from the hips with their knees a little flexed but with their back as straight as it would be for a longer shot. You should feel as if your hands are hanging directly down from your shoulders. It is also important to keep your grip light because any tension at address will be replicated throughout the swing.

HOW TO PLAY THE BASIC CHIP

This is the shot you should use when you find yourself just off a green with no trouble between you and the flag. It is sometimes called the bump and run, and for good reason because it is designed to be played predominantly along the ground. The basic chip shot can be played with anything between a 7-iron and a wedge, depending on the terrain between your ball and the hole.

The idea of the shot is to fly the ball onto a flat piece of ground in front of you and then let the ball run on towards the hole. It can be used to get over the fringe of a green and is also particularly useful on seaside courses where the ground is hard and ideally suited to a running shot.

The technique used for a chip shot is similar to the technique used for a basic pitch, and it remains the same irrespective of the club you choose to use.

The stance is the first thing that mirrors that used in the pitch. You will see from the photographs that my shoulders are square to the target but my feet are a little open. The ball is a little back in my stance. My hands are well forward and about 70 per cent of my weight is on my left side. The position I adopt at address means that I will be hitting down on the ball and this is reinforced by the swing I use.

When hitting a chip shot, my weight will remain on my left side throughout the swing. The swing itself is predominantly a hand and arm movement in which the wrists remain passive at all times. The distance you hit the ball is governed by the length of your backswing, which can sometimes be a source of problems for amateur golfers. The tendency is to swing back too far and then decelerate into the ball, so you will have to experiment until you get a feel for what you should be doing. Bear in mind that the length of your through swing should be about the same as your backswing. But also remember that your hands should never pass your club head. That would result in a scoop and all manner of bad results.

In my experience, good chippers will try to hole almost every chip they play. To do that, they will study the contours of the green just as closely as if they were putting. They will pick a spot on which they want to land the ball, take a few practice swings to get a feel for the shot, and then make an aggressive pass at the ball. In contrast, poor chippers seem almost resigned to failure. They grab the first club that comes to hand, take little or no note of the contours of the green, and get the shot over and done with as soon as possible.

CHOOSING WHICH CLUB TO USE

Arguably the most difficult aspect of a bump-and-run shot is deciding which club to use. This requires a certain amount of visualisation and also a basic understanding of what the ball will do when it hits the ground.

When I am about to hit a chip shot, the first thing I do is move to the side and survey the terrain I have in front of me. I am looking for a flat piece of ground to land the ball on, and that in turn will govern which club I select. Under normal circumstances I will use a 7-iron, 9-iron or wedge for this sort of shot. I will use the 7-iron if I want the ball to fly 25 per cent of the distance and then roll the rest of the way to the flag. I will select a 9-iron if I want the ball to fly 50 per cent and a wedge if I want to carry the shot 75 per cent of the way to the hole. I should add these are rough guides and will differ according to the prevailing conditions. On a links course, for example, the ball will tend to roll further than it would on a softer, inland course. Likewise, on a course with grain on the greens, the ball will roll significantly further down grain than it will against the grain. If you are playing on a course other than your own, it pays to practise these shots, just to get a feel for what happens.

THE DOWNHILL CHIP

When faced with a downhill chip, many golfers automatically reach for a 5-iron, hoping it will help them to trundle the ball down the hill and onto the green. For me, though, that is the wrong choice, because it will create too much topspin, making it difficult for you to stop your ball at, or around, the hole. Here, the problem is exactly the opposite to the one you will encounter when faced with the uphill chip. Normally, a 5-iron has between 28 to 30 degrees of loft, but when you factor in a 35-degree slope, like the one pictured here, all of a sudden you are using a club with negative loft.

In this scenario, I tend to select one of my wedges, thereby enabling me to get the ball into the air and providing a bit of stop. I will also play the ball a bit further forward in my stance than normal, ensuring that my weight remains on my front foot throughout the swing.

As with the other chip shots I have mentioned, I try to keep my wrists as quiet as possible on this shot. The worst thing you can do is to try to scoop the ball into the air, as this will cause you to thin the shot or hit it fat. So concentrate instead on making a rhythmical movement with your arms, letting the loft on the club do the work for you.

When hitting a downhill chip, it is even more important than normal to keep your head down well after you have made contact with the ball. If you don't, you will almost certainly hit the ground behind the ball, causing you to duff it, or thin the ball through the green. It is also important to commit to the shot. If you decelerate, the chances are you won't get the ball anywhere near the hole.

THE UPHILL CHIP

Sometimes I will select a club other than the 7-iron, 9-iron or wedge if I believe my lie requires it. One such scenario is when I am faced with an uphill chip. Whenever you are on a slope, your first consideration has to be whether the slope is severe enough to add, or subtract, loft from your club face. If it is, you will need to proceed accordingly.

Faced with an uphill slope, many amateur golfers reach for a wedge or a sand wedge, hoping to flick the ball into the air. All too often, though, the ball comes to rest well short of the target, leaving a long putt to save par. The reason for this is that the upslope adds loft to the club. On a severe slope, like the one pictured here, a 48-degree wedge will suddenly play like a 60-degree wedge. Of course, realising this, you could simply hit the shot a little harder. That might well work but, instead, I normally choose a 9-iron, or even an 8-iron, thereby keeping the ball a little lower to the ground and ensuring that it rolls out towards the hole. I try to swing with the upslope rather than fighting against it. For that reason, I will start with a bit more weight on my right side than normal and will also move the ball a little bit back in my stance. From this position, I concentrate on swinging normally, keeping the club face square, and following through up the slope.

THE 3-WOOD CHIP

This is a shot that has become quite popular on the Tour during the last few years. Tiger Woods and David Duval were among the first to use it, but it has now been copied by a lot of other pros.

The 3-wood chip is an ideal shot if you are close to the green but too far away to use a putter. But don't even attempt it if your ball is more than four feet from the putting surface or if it is lying in deep rough.

This shot is basically a putt with a 3-wood. The loft on the club ensures that the ball will carry over the fringe but then land and roll out just like a normal putt.

Grip the club well down the shaft, using either your normal grip or a conventional putting grip, and sweep the club head back low so that it brushes the top of the grass. Then concentrate on accelerating the club head through the ball, hitting it with about the same force as you would with a putt from a similar distance.

THE TEXAS WEDGE

There are many golfers out there who believe that a putter can only be used on a green, but nothing could be further from the truth. Sometimes, when the ground is hard, making the use of a broad-soled club difficult, using a putter from off the green represents the safest option. Certainly, it is an option always worth considering.

The term Texas wedge originated in the Lone Star State, where I went to university and where the wind is invariably a factor. Nowadays, however, it is a shot used most often on a traditional British links.

Regular visitors to the Old Course, St Andrews, will have seen this shot played many times. Some locals, for example, like to use the Texas wedge when approaching the ninth green because the terrain is dead flat and distances are difficult to judge. Others see it as a preferred option when the hole is cut on the shelf at the back of the twelfth green.

In the end, it is about going with a shot you feel comfortable with. It is also about percentages. If you feel that seven times out of ten you will get the ball closer to the hole with a putter than with another club, then use it. You would be daft not to. As the old saying goes, 'it is not how, but how many'.

THE HIGH LOB

This is a shot required when playing to a tight pin placement, where you have very little green to work with. It is a dangerous shot and difficult to play under pressure, but can produce sensational results. It is basically a soft shot, made with a fullish, slow-motion swing. The flop shot, as played by Phil Mickelson and one or two others, uses much more club-head speed but is even more dangerous and best left to the experts.

When I am playing a high lob shot, I use a three-quarter-length swing but one that generates about half the speed of a normal shot. It is a gentle arm swing, with restricted body movement and very little leg action. At address, my shoulders, hips and feet are all open and about 60 per cent of my weight is on my back foot. The ball is well forward in my stance and the face of my lob wedge is open. In contrast to most shots, my hands might even be a little behind the ball.

For this shot, the backswing is long, the through swing much less so. What I am attempting is literally to slide the club face under the ball at impact. I try to hold the club face open through impact, concentrating on keeping it pointing to the sky at the finish of the swing. The desired result is a very high, soft shot that stops almost as soon as it hits the green. But it requires practice and should not be contemplated unless there is a bit of give in the ground.

7

There is no doubt that many amateur golfers are absolutely terrified of playing bunker shots. I have seen numerous pro-am partners reduced to gibbering wrecks when faced with a straightforward bunker shot. This is strange when you consider Tour professionals believe the basic bunker shot is among the easiest shots in golf.

How to Succeed from Sand

There is a simple reason for this divergence of opinion which stems from the fact that Tour professionals understand what is required to get a golf ball out of sand while the average amateur does not. All too often an amateur will jump into a bunker with no real idea about what he needs to do to extricate his ball from the sand. He is resigned to failure and so is not surprised when the result is poor.

In this chapter I want to teach you the mechanics of a sound sand stroke. You will see that the techniques required differ from those needed for other golf shots, but they are easily mastered and should allow you to lose your fear of sand.

THE SPLASH SHOT

SETTING UP

This is my stock shot for getting out of greenside bunkers. It is similar to the high lob I described in Chapter 6, but I think you will find it easier to execute once you understand how it works.

The secret to hitting good bunker shots is to get yourself set up correctly. You are aiming to get the ball into the air as quickly as possible, and to do that there are several steps you have to take.

The first thing to do is to make sure that you set up with your feet, hips and shoulders all aiming to the left of the target (see right), which will encourage you to swing from out-to-in, and will help you to impart slice spin on the ball. You also need to open up the face of your sand wedge and to dig your feet into the sand. The latter has three benefits. It gives you a solid base in a loose surface. It gives you a feel for the texture of the sand. And it helps you to hit the sand first by lowering the base of your swing arc below the level of the ball.

When I play this shot, I set myself up so that the ball is in line with my left heel. That is two or three inches to the left of where I would normally hit an iron from, but it ensures that my club face will hit the sand first and slide under the ball.

Setting yourself up correctly is vital to good bunker play, and the last piece in the puzzle is to get your weight distribution right. I have about 80 to 90 per cent of my weight on my left side because that encourages me to pick up the club sharply and promotes a steeper and more positive swing.

I have found that many amateurs do not understand what they have to do to open up their sand wedge, so let me show you how to do it.

Prior to getting into the bunker, ground your sand wedge and then turn the leading edge of the club to the right from twelve o'clock to about two o'clock. That, in a nutshell, is all you have to do to open the club head. The further you turn the club head, the more loft you create.

But a word of warning: never attempt this routine once you are in the bunker. The Rules of Golf forbid this, a golfer incurring a two-shot penalty if he grounds his sand wedge, or even touches the sand with the club head, prior to hitting a bunker shot.

EXECUTING THE SPLASH SHOT

Once you have got yourself set up correctly, you are 75 per cent of the way there. Next you have to pick the spot in the sand where you want the club to enter and commit yourself to the shot. I have aligned myself so that I am about 30 degrees open (or to the left of the target) and now all I do is swing where my body is aiming. That will produce an outside-to-in swing path and will create the sort of cut spin I am looking for. The length of my backswing will vary, depending on the texture of the sand and the distance I have to hit the ball, but it is important not to take the club too far back. One of the most common mistakes made by poor bunker players is to decelerate into the ball, and that is often caused by too long a backswing.

I like to be aggressive when I hit this shot. I want to explode the ball out of the sand, but at the same time I want it to land softly, so I make sure that the face of my sand wedge remains open right to the end of my swing. This is something we looked at when describing the high lob shot. It might sound somewhat complicated, but it is easily done. Just concentrate on keeping your club face pointing to the sky during the follow through and you will achieve what you set out to do.

HOW MUCH SAND SHOULD I TAKE?

This is a question I am asked a lot during pro-ams, but I am afraid there is no one simple answer. It all depends on the texture of the sand in the bunkers and also on how much spin you want to put on the ball when it lands. Experimentation is the only way to find an answer, although there are a number of guidelines to remember.

An ideal divot for a normal sand shot is long and shallow rather than short and deep. The club head will enter the sand anywhere between one and two inches behind the ball but will not resurface until at least three inches past the ball. What you are trying to do is blast the ball out on a cushion of sand. A good way to get a feel for what you are doing is to practise

bunker shots without a ball. Concentrate on taking long and shallow divots and remember to focus on the spot you want the club to enter the sand rather than on the ball itself.

I should add here that spin is another factor to consider when deciding how much sand to take. When faced with a shot in which there is not much room between the bunker and the hole, I might elect to take as little as three-quarters of an inch of sand as I know this will maximise the backspin I put on the ball. Conversely, when I want the ball to run, I will do the opposite. In this scenario I will aim for a spot as much as two to three inches behind the ball, knowing that the sand will cushion the impact and take most of the spin off the ball.

HOW TO SELECT A SUITABLE SAND WEDGE

The modern sand wedge has been designed specifically for the job it has to do. It is manufactured with the back of the sole closer to the ground than the leading edge, and this characteristic (often referred to as 'bounce') enables the club to cut through the sand rather than dig into it. Some sand wedges have more 'bounce' than others and so are suitable for different playing conditions.

When you come to purchase your next sand wedge, it is important to select a club that will perform well in the bunkers on the course where you play the majority of your golf.

When making the decision, bear in mind that sand wedges with little 'bounce' and narrow soles work best in firm sand. Conversely, clubs with lots of 'bounce' and wide soles are best for use in soft, fluffy sand.

I should add here that 'bounce' is also a factor to consider when buying utility wedges. Lower 'bounce' angles suit tight, hard fairways. Higher 'bounce' angles work better when the ground is soft and lush.

HOW TO ESCAPE FROM A BURIED LIE

There is nothing worse than arriving at a bunker and finding your ball plugged deep under the surface. But it does not necessarily spell disaster, provided you know what to do. There are two secrets to extricating your ball from this sort of situation. The first is to utilise the leading edge of your sand iron. The second is to refrain from getting too cute with the shot. The most important thing to do is to get the ball out of the bunker. Finesse does not come into it at all.

When faced with a shot like this, my stance will be a little more square than it would be for a more conventional greenside bunker shot (see right), and I make a couple of other important adjustments, too.

In order to create a steep downward blow, I address the ball with about 70 per cent of my weight on my left foot and with the ball situated about the middle of my stance. I also square up my club face, or even close it slightly, because this helps it to cut through the sand and it gets the club head under the ball.

At the start of the backswing, I will break my wrists early, make a shortish backswing, and then drive the club down into the sand about half an inch behind the ball. Unusually in golf, I won't have much of a follow through when hitting this shot. Instead, the through swing is truncated (see main picture). This shot is all about creating sufficient club-head speed to blast the ball out of its crater. But remember that you will not be able to produce any backspin, so the ball will run a long way when it lands.

CHIPPING FROM SAND

Most golfers automatically reach for their sand wedge when they find their ball in a bunker, but sometimes that is not necessarily the best choice of club. There will be an odd occasion when it might be possible to chip the ball out of the sand, although the conditions would have to be absolutely right before you would even contemplate this shot.

I would never attempt this shot unless I had both a perfect lie and little or no lip to come over. You would also require a lot of room between the edge of the bunker and the hole, because a chip from

sand will take longer to stop than a similar chip from grass.

The chip from sand has a number of advantages, not the least of which is that it is easier to know how hard (or soft) to swing than it is with a more conventional bunker shot.

It also requires less precision to produce an acceptable result.

When you decide to take this shot on, you have to set up with your feet a little open and with the ball an inch or so behind the centre of your stance. You need to make sure the club you use has

enough loft to get the ball over the lip of the bunker but not so much that it results in you running into trouble on the other side of the green.

I would suggest that you practise with a number of different clubs to see how the ball reacts. The most important thing to remember is to keep your hands and wrists firmish throughout the shot. Make sure you do not break your wrists too much because, if you do, the club head will hit the sand before the ball, invariably resulting in the ball staying in the bunker.

HOW TO PLAY A FAIRWAY BUNKER SHOT

The first thing you should do when you find yourself in a fairway bunker is make a realistic assessment of your position. There will be some occasions when you will be able to achieve a good deal of distance out of the bunker, but others when all you can do is get the ball out.

When the bunker is shallow and the lie is good, as it is in the example shown in the photographs, the objective is to get the ball as far out of the bunker as possible. It almost goes without saying that the one thing you must not do when hitting a long bunker shot is hit the ball heavy. This is the one time when hitting the ball a little thin can be beneficial, so you have to set yourself up accordingly.

When I am faced with a shot like this, I stand square to the target but with a little more weight on my left side than normal. I make sure I dig my feet about half an inch into the sand, but also compensate for this loss of height by holding the club a similar distance from the top of the grip. When playing this shot, is it vital that you retain your height throughout the swing. I focus on a point just above the equator of the golf ball and then try to keep my hips level throughout the swing.

This shot is played mainly with the hands and arms, so the chances are that you will need at least one more club than you would from a similar shot off grass. Swing nice and slow and try to pick the ball cleanly off the sand.

WHEN TO PLAY SAFE IN A FAIRWAY BUNKER

Unfortunately, when the lie is poor (as shown), or the bunker is very deep, you will be unable to get distance from a fairway bunker. When you find yourself in this position it is important to be realistic. Forget the heroics. Instead, treat it like a normal explosion shot and get the ball out as best you can.

When in this position, I revert to the technique shown on pages 142 and 143. I open my stance,

open my club face and drive the club under the ball, extricating it along with the sand around about it. Remember, it is important to be aggressive with this shot. Hit down hard into the sand about an inch or so behind the ball. Get it out at all costs, accept a dropped shot, and then try to get your next shot onto the green.

PART 3 THE MENTAL GAME

Over the years I have lost count of the number of times I have come across amateur golfers who hit the ball well but score badly. It is a widespread problem but can easily be overcome if the golfers in question learn how to improve their thinking on the golf course.

How to Play Smart Golf

I have always said that I could save an average amateur golfer five or six shots a round if I caddied for him, and this is no idle boast. The simple fact of the matter is that if I acted as your caddie I would help you to eradicate the mental errors that are often the root cause of poor scores.

I cannot stress enough how important it is to learn how to think your way round a golf course. Sound course management can often mean the difference between a good score and a bad one. Poor course management will invariably mean that you will not fulfil your potential.

When I play golf, I leave absolutely nothing to chance. Everything is deliberated carefully. Unfortunately, far too many amateurs are much more cavalier in their approach to the game. Successful businessmen, trained to process all sorts of information before making a decision, seem to lose this ability to analyse as soon as they step onto a golf course. Instead, they switch on to automatic pilot, seldom stopping to consider the consequences of the shot they are about to play.

Much of what follows is, I admit, nothing more than mere common-sense. However, I make no apologies for this, because failure to adopt a common-sense approach to your golf is potentially just as ruinous as a poor grip or faulty set-up. Famously, Jack Nicklaus once said that golf was 10 per cent physical and 90 per cent mental, and he was right, of course. Put another way, you can have the best swing in the world but you will not become a winner until you learn to think your way round a golf course.

CHAPTER

BEFORE YOU TEE UP

WARM UP PROPERLY

When you arrive at the golf course, the first thing you should do is give yourself a chance to play decent golf. When possible, you should give yourself time to warm up prior to a round of golf, not just to get your muscles moving, but to flush the last vestiges of your working day out of your system. There are many exercises you can do, but one of the best is to swing two clubs at once (see photo). Begin swinging in a leisurely fashion, then slowly build up to full speed as and when you feel you are loosening up. It's a great way to get the muscles moving.

Once loosened up, it also makes sense to hit a few shots. I have developed a twenty-six-shot warm-up routine that I suggest all golfers should adopt prior to going out on the golf course. It is a marvellous way to loosen up, but does not take much time.

Once I arrive at the practice ground, I begin by doing a few gentle stretching exercises. One of my favourites is to put a club head in the crook of one elbow, place the shaft behind my back, and then put the other end of the club in the crook of my other elbow. Once I am in this position, I rotate my upper body, first one way, then the other, just as I would during a golf swing.

Having loosened up, I will make a few leisurely practice swings before hitting some balls. I start by hitting two sand wedges, then two wedges, two 9-irons, and so on, until I have hit two shots with every club in the bag. Sometimes, if I have time, I will then reverse the process, hitting two drivers, two 3-woods, and so on, all the way down to my sand wedge again.

By the time I am finished, I feel nice and loose. From there, I move onto the practice putting green, where I hit a few putts to get a feel for the greens, before finishing off with a couple of practice bunker shots.

PARK YOUR PROBLEMS

Good golf starts not when you step onto the first tee but long before, often when you get up in the morning. Prior to a round, it is important to stay relaxed. Try not to let anything upset you, because, if you are flustered, it will be reflected in your scores. Often, of course, this is impossible, particularly if you have had a tough day at the office prior to starting a round. In those circumstances, try to blank out your business problems before you even get out

of your car. Certainly, you do not want to take them onto the golf course with you, because, once you tee up, you have to concentrate 100 per cent on your game. Warm up as described on the opposite page.

When possible, try to get to the course well ahead of your allotted tee-time. Take time out to talk with friends, have a soft drink, or read a magazine. In other words, relax, because you will never play good golf if you feel on edge.

PLAY THE FIRST TEE SHOT IN YOUR HEAD

Over the years, countless golfers have told me they hate hitting their first tee shot of the day. In fact, I have lost count of the times I have seen amateurs hit a poorish shot off the first tee and then mumble something along the lines of, 'Well, at least that's the first shot over and done with.' If you are one of those people, I recommend you 'play' your first tee shot in your head a few times before you leave the practice ground. To do this, select your driver, or whichever club you feel most comfortable with. Next, stand behind the ball, just as you would as part of your normal pre-shot routine, and visualise the shot you want to hit. If you hit a good shot, it will give you a great deal of confidence when you come to tee off. If not, try another, until you are satisfied with the result.

Finally, if all else fails and you still arrive at the first tee feeling apprehensive, why not leave the driver in your bag? Select a club you feel more comfortable with, relax and tee off.

CISCO
WORLD MATCH PLAY CHAMPIONSHIP

1

473 YDS   PAR 4

cisco.com

CISCO SYSTEMS

cisco.co

LEARN TO USE THE TEEING GROUND TO YOUR BEST ADVANTAGE

When hitting a shot from the tee, take some time to work out the best place to tee up. As a general rule, if you fade the ball, as I do, I recommend you should tee up on the right edge of the teeing ground and aim down the left side of the fairway (see right). That way, you have 100 per cent of the fairway to aim at. Conversely, if you normally hit a draw,

tee up on the left and aim down the right. Remember, if you want to exaggerate this, the Rules permit you to stand with your feet *outside* the tee markers, provided that the ball is between the markers.

On particularly difficult holes, it makes sense to tee up so that you are playing away from the worst of the

trouble. If, for example, a water hazard runs down the right-hand side of the fairway, tee your ball up on the right. Conversely, if there is a group of bunkers eating into the landing area down the left, stand on the left side of the teeing ground.

STICK TO YOUR GAME PLAN ON EACH HOLE

Back in 1993, I played with Nick Faldo in the Ryder Cup foursomes and four-balls, and he taught me a valuable lesson, one that I have never forgotten. He impressed on me that there is a 'right' and a 'wrong' way to play each hole. In practice, he worked out exactly what he thought was the 'right' way to tackle each of the eighteen holes on the Brabazon Course at the Belfry, and then he stuck to that game plan, regardless of what the opposition was doing or the state of the match.

As far as I am concerned, amateurs would be well advised to adopt a similar strategy. Instead of stepping onto a tee and reaching automatically for your driver, why not take a moment or two to assess what lies before you? Do that, and you will often find that you are reaching for a different club instead.

On this hole, for example, a short par four at the Wisley, it immediately becomes clear that there is insufficient room to hit a driver. Every now and then, I suppose, you *could* get lucky and find the fairway past the right-hand bunker, but, much more often, you would simply run through the fairway and find yourself in all sorts of trouble. By taking some time out to assess the lie of the land, you will soon see that an iron hit into the right-hand side of the fairway represents the safest option. From there, you will have no more than 120 yards into the green, giving yourself a realistic birdie chance.

FORWARD PLANNING

CHECK THE WIND DIRECTION
There are few more frustrating
experiences in golf than watching a
perfectly struck shot run through a
fairway or land short of a green.
Inevitably, of course, we all choose the
wrong club from time to time, but you
can cut down on these errors if you
check the direction of the wind prior to
hitting each shot. To do this, simply
throw some grass in the air and watch its
speed and direction as it blows away
(right). If you watch the pros in action,
you will see them doing this, if not
before every shot, then certainly regularly
throughout the round.

This is a good habit to adopt, but
remember to take your surroundings into
consideration when doing it. If, for
example, you are close to a copse of trees,
it may well be that the wind will be
diminished. In this scenario, it makes sense
to observe the tops of the trees to see if
they are being blown more. This will give
you a good idea of what your ball will
encounter once it gets into the air.

MAKE YOUR MARK
While on the subject of getting into
good habits, it is important to mark your
golf ball prior to the start of the round.
Otherwise, if you have the misfortune to
find two similar balls side by side and are
unable to identify which is yours, you
will have to deem the ball to be lost and
will be penalised stroke and distance.
The manufacturer prints my special
mark for me (opposite page). You will
need to choose how you want to mark
your ball and then write it on every ball
you use.

Do Not Turn One Bad Shot into Two

One key to avoiding a high score is never to follow a bad shot with a bad decision. If, for example, you find yourself in trees, do not attempt to go for the miracle escape shot (see above), which might come off one time in a hundred. Instead, accept a dropped shot and concentrate on getting back onto the fairway by the simplest route (see left).

In my experience, amateurs tend to be too aggressive when playing out of the rough, attempting to extricate their ball with a 5-wood or a long iron when using a short iron would be a much more sensible play. Unfortunately, going for the big shot invariably leads to more problems, and an even higher score.

ASSESS THE RISK

In America, when a pin is hidden behind a bunker, or close to a hazard, they call it a 'sucker pin'. This is an apt description because only a sucker would go for it. Sometimes, of course, if you go for the pin, you will succeed in getting close enough to secure a birdie, but usually you will hit your ball into serious trouble and run up a bogey or a double-bogey instead.

So when faced with a sucker pin it is much better to play the percentage shot: ignore the pin and aim for a more accessible part of the green. That way, you may have a tougher putt for a birdie, but you'll also greatly reduce the risk of shooting a big number.

While on the subject of playing safe, it is worth pointing out that, on occasions, it might make sense not to go for the green at all, but rather deliberately lay up and then attempt to pitch and putt for a par. One hole where this is often the best option is the seventeenth at Valderrama, venue for the annual Volvo Masters and the 1997 Ryder Cup (right). On this hole, you have next to no margin for error when you are hitting your shot to the green. Given that that is the case, if you find your drive out of position, even by a yard or two, it is often better to lay up short of the water and then try to get up and down from there.

PUTTING A SCORE TOGETHER

DON'T BE AFRAID
TO COMPILE A GOOD SCORE

How familiar does this scenario sound? You're putting together a good round: you're swinging smoothly, pitching and putting well. Then you look at your scorecard (above), see you are four shots under your handicap ... and panic.

Invariably, in a situation like this, you start to play defensively, don't you? I know this because I've done it myself.

Instead of trusting your swing, you try to steer your drives, become a little cautious with your irons and begin to lag your putts. All of a sudden, your run of good scoring comes to an end.

When you find yourself in this situation, the best advice I can give is don't try to protect your score. Stay aggressive. Tell yourself you are swinging well. In other words, trust and let go.

ALLOW FOR A MISHIT

In golf, as in the rest of life, it pays to be realistic. Nobody, not even a top golfer, strikes the ball perfectly every time. So, especially if you're a newcomer to the game, you have to expect to mishit the ball more. My philosophy is that you should allow for your mishits by taking an extra club. That's smart course management and will often help you to reduce your scores.

While on the subject of clubbing, I cannot help but think that most amateurs would be well advised to be much more realistic about the distance they can hit the ball. Henry Cotton, the former Open champion, used to say that the safest place to stand at an amateur event was right behind the flag, and he was right. If you don't believe me, just think back to your last round, and tell me how many full approach shots you hit past the hole. One? Two? I would be willing to bet it wasn't more than that.

LEARN TO USE YOUR SHOTS
I believe that the vast majority of amateur golfers could use their strokes much better than they do. If you are a 14-handicapper, for example, why go all out to get a par on the stroke-index on one hole when all you need is a bogey to play to your handicap? Likewise, if you have a shot on a hole, why try to get cute with a difficult bunker shot (see photo)? Almost invariably, if you try to get the ball close to the pin in this sort of scenario, you will leave the ball in the sand, thereby running the risk of carding a double-bogey or worse. Instead, why not make sure you get the ball out? Hit it to the far side of the green, take two putts, and escape with a net par.

PLAY THE PERCENTAGES

It's a fact of life that no matter how accurate you are off the tee, you're going to land in the rough every now and then. That's inevitable, I'm afraid, although you can help to cut down the risk by being conservative with your choice of club. Even on a long par four, it is not essential for you to use a driver from the tee, particularly if the fairway is narrow, or if there is trouble in the landing zone. In this sort of scenario, it would be much more sensible to try to hit, say, a 3-iron followed by a 6-iron, rather than the driver and a 9-iron.

In the same way, don't be afraid to play deliberately short at a long par three if you are worried about making the carry. After all, why run the risk of ending up in a water hazard or a cavernous bunker when you could play short, pitch on and leave yourself a short one-putt for par?

ELIMINATE YOUR DISASTER SHOT

If you are a low handicapper, your good shots are probably just as good as mine. We differ, though, in our poor shots: mine are bad, whereas yours are potentially disastrous. For example, your Achilles' heel might be a huge, high slice, while mine is a gentle pull. Your bad shots end up in the trees, while mine drift to the edge of the fairway or into the semi-rough.

The key to improving is to identify your problem shot and then find a way to reduce its ill-effects. Often, of course, this will require a lesson with a PGA pro, followed by a series of practice sessions. Not always, though. Sometimes, when thinking about your bad shots, you will realise there is a common factor. Maybe they always happen when you try to get a bit of extra distance. Perhaps your biggest disasters occur when you try to steer the ball. Armed with this sort of information, you could be well on the way to effecting a cure.

LEARN FROM WHAT YOU SEE

When on a golf course, it frequently pays dividends to watch and learn from your partners. If, for example, you have a similar putt to someone else in your group, it would be madness not to watch to see how the ball reacts (above). Likewise, on the tee of a par three, it does no harm to look to see what club your partner is using. However, whatever you do, do not ask him outright, as this would be deemed as asking for advice and would result in a two-shot penalty.

Observing your partner is useful out on the course, and it is equally important to find someone whose opinion you trust to help you when your game is out of sorts. But do not get into the habit of taking advice from all and sundry, however well meaning that advice might be. 'Too many cooks spoil the broth'

is as true in golf as it is in anything else. I have lost count of the number of times I have seen struggling golfers attempt to elicit advice from several different sources, only to find themselves suffering from paralysis by analysis (above). Nine times out of ten, the cause of your problems will be easily spotted by someone who knows your game well. Trust their judgement, and politely decline advice from all other sources.

EACH SHOT DESERVES YOUR FULL ATTENTION

It never ceases to amaze me the number of times I see amateur golfers rush up to a shot and then hit it, seemingly without thinking about it first. In pro-ams I see it happening constantly, almost always with disastrous results.

When I am playing golf, I like to think that I concentrate fully on each and every shot I hit. Walking towards the ball, I will size up the shot to assess the options I have. Once I get to it, I will discuss the yardage with my caddie, check the wind direction and any other factors that might affect the shot. Only when I am sure I am absolutely ready will I pull a club from my bag and start my pre-swing routine.

I think it makes sense to pick out an explicit target every time you hit a shot. Don't just aim for the fairway or the green. Pick out a tree or a hump in the fairway, and then focus all your attention on hitting towards that spot.

COMMIT TO THE SHOT

Choosing a club can sometimes be difficult, especially when the wind is gusting or the shot requires considerable accuracy. When this is the case, it pays to take your time before you decide whether you should be hitting, say, a 3-iron or a 4-iron. Having said that, I think you will find that more often than not your first choice is the right one. Certainly, in my experience, that's the case.

Then it is important to commit to the club you have selected. If you have doubts in your mind about your club selection, the chances are you will swing tentatively, resulting in a poor shot. So be positive. Select a club, push any doubts about it from your mind, and swing as aggressively as you can.

ELEVATION WILL ALTER YOUR CLUB SELECTION

When on the golf course, it is not just the wind and the temperature that can affect your club selection. Elevation changes must also be considered.

When you are hitting a shot downhill, the chances are you will need less club than for a similar shot uphill. An example of this is the eleventh at Valderrama (pictured). It measures 197 yards, which normally for me would mean hitting a 4-iron, but, because it is downhill, I normally hit a club less. In contrast, when I am left with, say, a 160-yard shot to a green set 10 yards above me, I will normally select one club more than I would have done if I didn't have to climb to reach the green.

Selecting the right club to suit changes in elevation comes with experience. However, as a general rule, if there is a 10-yard drop (or rise), you will need one club less (or more), and if there is a 20-yard drop (or rise), you will need two clubs less (or more).

TAKE THE POSITIVES FROM YOUR ROUND

Sadly, no matter how good a player you are, there will always be times when you come off the course disappointed with your round. That's inevitable, I'm afraid. Not even Tiger Woods plays well all the time, although I have to admit he seems to manage it more than most.

When you have had a bad round, it is important for you to sit down and work out why you dropped the shots you did. Was it primarily due to bad driving? Did your irons let you down? Was your course management poor? If you can find the answers to these questions, you will know what to work on ahead of your next round.

So it is important to isolate your weaknesses, but don't stop there. You also have to home in on the positives. Of course, you might have done some things badly, but, equally, the chances are you will also have done something else rather well. When analysing your rounds, it is important to congratulate yourself. Learning to take the positives out of a round is something Hugh Mantle, a lecturer in sports psychology at John Moores University in Liverpool, taught me, and it works, I can assure you. It helps to keep things in perspective and means that the next time you tee up, you won't be quite as apprehensive as you might otherwise have been.

CHAPTER

In golf, there are three different types of practice. There is the warm-up, which should be done before the start of each round. There is the practice session, designed to cure a specific swing fault. And there is the session in which the main goal is to maintain what you have got already.

Make the Most of Your Practice

Earlier, in Chapter 8, I gave you my thoughts on the best ways to warm up. Here, I want to offer you some advice on how to get the most from the other two types of practice session. There is an old adage that suggests that 'practice makes perfect'. Like most adages, it is correct, but only up to a point.

Sadly, all too often, amateur golfers reap little or no benefit from their practice because they practise poorly, setting out with the wrong goals, or rushing through the session, taking no time to think about what they are doing. So here is some simple, common-sense advice that should stop you falling into that trap.

TAKE LESSONS FROM A PGA PROFESSIONAL

I am a great believer in Gary Player's theory that 'the more you practise, the luckier you get', but only if you know what you are trying to accomplish. All too often, amateur golfers go to the range with little or no idea about what they should be working on and consequently fail to make much progress. It seems to me to be a complete waste of time to spend hours hitting golf balls if you do not have a clue about what you need to work on to make your golf better. No sensible businessman would ever start a new enterprise without a sound business plan, so why should a golfer go to the range without a clear practice plan in place?

I recommend that all amateur golfers who want to improve should start by investing in a couple of lessons from a PGA professional. I would also suggest that you make regular return visits to the pro of your choice, because it is easy to fall into bad habits without realising you have done so.

I have been fortunate over the years to have had a number of excellent coaches who have been able to pinpoint my swing problems and make recommendations about what I need to do to improve. The result is that each time I go to the range I have a clear picture of exactly what I am trying to accomplish. It takes longer to iron out a problem on some occasions than on others, but at least I know I am channelling my energies in the right direction and am not wasting my time trying to mend something that does not need to be fixed.

I am a great believer in seeking advice from experts. But it is worth adding a word of caution here: it is important to be selective in what you listen to. More than one leading golfer has tied himself in knots by listening to advice from all and sundry. So ask around to find out who is the best pro in your area and then ignore advice from everybody else.

DISTINGUISH BETWEEN PRACTICE AND WARMING UP

On a competition day, I never go to the range to practise. I'm there purely to warm up, stretch my muscles and find myself some rhythm.

It's important to distinguish between practice and warming up and to realise that a tournament day is not the time to tinker with your swing. After all, it takes time to bed in even the smallest of swing changes, and, while you are going through this process, it would be unrealistic to expect good results.

If you want to work on improving your game, fine, just don't try to do it in the hours leading up to an important medal round. That sort of work should be done early in the week at the driving range, not on a Saturday or Sunday twenty minutes before you tee off.

ALWAYS HAVE A TARGET IN MIND

Without wishing to sound too simplistic, it is worth pointing out that you should always aim at a target whenever you are working on your game. I have lost count of the times that I have stood on a practice ground and watched as amateurs bashed balls about without any thought to where they were hitting them. Most driving ranges have targets and I strongly advise you to use them.

Once you are warmed up (right) as described on page 160, start by hitting shots to the nearest target, which is normally about 50 yards away. Then move up to the 100-yard marker, the 150-yard marker, and so on. The idea is to hit every single shot to a target. That's important because, if you don't do it, you won't know how accurately you are hitting the ball.

Once you have been through the bag, hitting shots right through from your wedges to your driver, I think it is a good idea to jump from one target to another, say from the 175-yard marker to the 75-yard marker and then up to the 200-yard marker. You can even make a game of it, not switching until you have hit three shots directly at the target you were aiming at. Accuracy is one of the key skills you need to play good golf. But it does not materialise by magic. You have to work on it and it is much better to do it on the range rather than on the course itself.

EACH SHOT IS IMPORTANT

TAKE YOUR TIME

It never ceases to amaze me the speed at which some amateurs get through a bucket of practice balls. In some cases, it seems almost to be a race to see who can finish quickest. Little or no thought goes into the session and the end result is that it does no good at all.

When I am practising, I like to take my time. I will start by doing a few gentle stretches, then take several practice swings, before going on to hit some leisurely wedges. Slowly but surely, I will go through the bag, hitting a few shots with each club. But it is not a continuous process, because I stop regularly,

either to evaluate what I am doing or simply to talk to a caddie or one of the other pros on the range.

What you have to remember is that each practice shot is important, irrespective of whether you are warming up or attempting to sort out a particular swing problem. It needs all your concentration and must not be hurried, as this will have a detrimental effect on the results.

One more piece of advice about practising: never hit shots when you feel tired. Tired swings can create bad habits. And bad habits, once ingrained, are often extremely difficult to iron out.

CHECK YOUR DIVOTS

I can understand why most golfers find it easier to practise at a driving range rather than on a traditional practice ground, but I believe it is a worthwhile exercise to hit practice shots off grass from time to time.

The reason for this is that you can learn a great deal about your swing from the shape of your divots. For example, if your divots curve left of the target, you probably have a classic slicer's swing, and will need to work on developing a more in-to-out action. Conversely, if your divots point right, the chances are

you hook the ball and so need to learn to swing more out-to-in.

You can also learn a lot from the depth of your divots. When you are swinging well, your divots will be long and shallow. If, however, you are hitting shots 'fat', you might have to check your posture or ball position. Equally, if you are hitting your shots 'thin', taking little or no divot, you could be coming up on the ball on the downswing.

Check to see if a common pattern emerges. If so, the best idea might be to consult your PGA pro. He or she will quickly spot the problem, and be able to recommend a cure.

MAKE THINGS AS SIMPLE FOR YOURSELF AS POSSIBLE

It is not easy to make major swing changes, so you owe it to yourself to make the process as simple as possible. When you are working on a big change, it is important to use one of your more playable clubs. I would recommend using a 7-iron or an 8-iron and would also suggest that you hit all of your shots off a tee (left).

To begin with, it is important not to be too concerned about where the ball is going. You should be concentrating on the swing position you are trying to get yourself into and should only start thinking about the target once that new position starts to feel natural.

It is also very important not to attempt to make too many changes at one time. This is a cardinal error that lots of amateur golfers fall into and has to be avoided at all costs. A good professional will give you no more than one or two swing changes to work on at any one time and will only progress onto others once he is sure those changes have been assimilated. That is a system you should also adopt, even if you decide to do all the work by yourself.

It also pays to be realistic when it comes to gauging your rate of progress. Don't get upset if you feel your game is not improving as fast as you think it should, particularly if you have embarked on major changes. 'Rome', as the say, 'was not built in a day', and neither is a golf swing. It takes time, and no little effort. Just ask Nick Faldo. He took two years to remodel his swing in the 1980s, but eventually it paid off when he won the Major titles he craved.

LEARN THE DISTANCE YOU HIT EACH CLUB

I cannot help but think that most amateur golfers would benefit a great deal from spending some time working out how far they hit each club in their bag. I understand that amateurs tend to be inconsistent when it comes to the distance they hit each club, but having some sort of benchmark still has to be much better than having none at all. All Tour pros see it as vital to know exactly how far they hit each club in their bag. I can tell you instantly what my own yardages are and this information is invaluable when it comes to selecting clubs out on the course.

It would pay big dividends to work out your own yardages.

The best way to do this is to find a quiet practice ground where you can do your measurements. A practice ground is better than a driving range because you can pace out your shots rather than rely on distance markers. A flat piece of ground is also essential because steep slopes will skew the results.

Start by spending some time warming up properly. Once you feel you are ready, pull out your wedge and hit ten full shots. In an ideal world, you will hit ten good ones into a tight circle, but if you do not, you should discount the worst ones and then jot down the average distance you have hit the rest. When you are happy that you have a realistic measurement, switch to a 9-iron and repeat the process. With a bit of luck you should be able to get a meaningful yardage from ten shots, but do not be afraid to hit more if you do not think those shots are representative of your average shots. The idea is to go through your bag, measuring the average distance you hit each club. You cannot hope to hit a club that distance every time you hit a shot with it, but at least it gives you something on which to base your club selection.

WORK ON YOUR WEAKNESSES

Human nature being what it is, when we go to the range, we often slip into the bad habit of practising what we are good at rather than concentrating on ironing out our weaknesses. Walk onto a range and you will see lots of amateur golfers hitting short irons and woods but not too many attempting to practise the long-iron shots that invariably cause them much more trouble out on the golf course.

Before you embark on a practice regime, it is important to analyse your strengths and weaknesses. You do not have to go as far as to keep statistics on fairways hit, greens in regulation and sand saves, like a lot of Tour professionals do, but you do have to have a fairly clear idea of what you are good at and what needs improving. Once you have isolated your weaknesses, it makes sense to work hardest on eradicating them. When the legendary Ben Hogan first turned professional, he was plagued by a terrible hook, but little by little, through sheer hard work, he overcame that problem and developed into one of the finest ball strikers the game has ever seen.

Through application, you can improve too, but you have to be realistic about what you can achieve, given the time restrictions placed on us. Most amateurs have neither the time nor the inclination to practise for eight hours a day. Some struggle to find more than an hour or two a week to practise. If you find yourself in the latter category, the secret is to utilise your time as best you can. Target your weaknesses sensibly and you will be surprised how much you can improve your scores.

I have always felt that amateurs who have little time to practise should spend most of what they have working on their short game rather than their long game. The reason for this is simple and it comes down to the shots you hit during a round of golf. During an average round, an 18-handicapper will hit fourteen drives and about the same number of fairway woods; and twenty to thirty full shots with his irons. He will hit many more shots on and around the green. So it stands to reason that the best way to lower your scores is to work on your short game. Realistically, an average amateur could save perhaps ten shots each round by improving his putting. He could also make a huge dent in his scores by practising his chipping and pitching. And that says nothing of the disasters you could avoid if you work on developing a sound technique in bunkers.

PRACTISE WITH A FRIEND

I recommend that, whenever possible, you should go to the practice range with a friend. The reason for this is twofold. First, and foremost, practice is a lot more fun if you have got somebody around to talk to. Second, your friend can give a second opinion, checking your aim, your posture, or whatever else you may be working on at a particular time. At the end of the session, the two of you can also have a competition, in which you take it in turns to get closest to the 50-yard, 100-yard or 150-yard marker. This is a great way to improve your accuracy. When doing it, I also recommend playing for a small wager, thereby recreating the sort of pressure you feel when you are out on the course.

This spring I got some first-hand experience of just how difficult it can be to find a set of clubs to suit your game. I had just changed my club contract from one company to another and it took me several months of trial and error before I was completely happy with the clubs I was using.

How to Choose the Right Equipment for You

I should state here and now that there was absolutely nothing wrong with the first clubs that the company gave me. They felt great when I picked them up but it was not until I switched to another model that I felt completely at ease.

This whole episode brought home to me how vital it is to find a set of clubs that suit your requirements. With the wrong set I can honestly say I was scoring five or six shots a round higher than I should have been. As soon as I switched to the other irons my score came down and my confidence started to return.

It is fair to say that few amateur golfers will have access to the range of equipment that I tested during those two or three months of experimentation, but that

should not stop you from shopping around. You are probably going to have to fork out upwards of £1,000 to obtain a premium set of clubs so you are entitled to try before you buy.

There is a lot to be said for going for a set of custom fit clubs (see page 200) but if you do not want to go down that road you should still test several different models before you make your final selection.

I would suggest that the first thing you do is to work out exactly what you want to spend and then get your professional to tell you what is available within that price range. You should be realistic when determining the limit to what you can and cannot spend. There's no point testing £500 drivers when you know you are going to have to settle for something costing less than half of that.

I would also recommend that you listen to your professional when it comes to selecting the sort of clubs you should be using. I will go into this in more detail over the next few pages. Suffice to say at present, if you are a mid-to-high-handicap golfer there's no point in setting your heart on the gleaming set of blades in the corner of the pro shop because even the pro himself would probably find them too difficult to use. Instead, check out the peripherally weighted irons. I promise you they are much easier to use.

One final thought before we move on. If you are a beginner, I would strongly recommend that you consider buying a second-hand set, at least until you decide the game is something you want to persevere with. You might even think about a half-set of irons, rather than a full set. Even for an experienced golfer, it is sometimes difficult to choose what club to use. For a beginner, therefore, it must be totally bewildering, particularly until you start to hit the ball consistently enough to be able to gauge how far you hit each club.

WHAT'S IN YOUR BAG?

The Rules of Golf stipulate that we are all allowed to carry a maximum of fourteen clubs in our golf bag at any one time. The secret is to find the right combination for you.

• DRIVER Most regular golfers will have noticed that drivers have changed a great deal over the last ten to fifteen years. At the start of the 1990s you still saw many persimmon drivers, but they have now all but disappeared to be replaced by hollow, lightweight, titanium drivers that are huge in comparison to the old wooden ones. This new breed of modern drivers gives all golfers some extra distance, but they really score by being much more forgiving than their persimmon predecessors. In the old days you lost a lot of distance if you did not make contact with the centre of the club face, but that is no longer the case. Peripheral weighting means that you can hit a drive out of the toe or the neck of the club and still generate reasonable distance.

The bad news is that this new technology comes at a price. A top-of-the-range driver can cost between £300 and £500, which makes it essential that you choose something suitable. I would recommend that you ask your professional to nominate what he believes are the most forgiving drivers in your price range, and then try them out to see which you like best. You should also be realistic when choosing a shaft. Most Tour professionals use extra stiff (XS) or stiff (S) shafts, but that doesn't mean they will be right for you. Unless you (a) are very strong and (b) generate lots of club-head speed, you should stick to regular (R) shafts for all of your clubs. OAPs should perhaps plump for something even softer.

• FAIRWAY WOODS Fairway woods have also changed a great deal over the years, and are now just as forgiving as the modern drivers. When you are purchasing your fairway woods, I would suggest you consider their loft, because there are big differences. Nowadays, the loft on a 3-wood can vary between 13 and 16 degrees, while other woods offer anything between 17 and 24 degrees.

It's best to go for a nice mix of lofts. If you use what I would describe as an average driver (with between 10 and 11 degrees of loft), I would recommend a 14–15-degree 3-wood and an 18-degree 5-wood. Golfers who find it difficult to hit their long irons might think about replacing them with a 7-wood. There are also 9-woods and 11-woods on the market.

It might be worthwhile testing the new breed of utility or rescue clubs. I have tried a couple and found they are as forgiving as a fairway wood but as accurate as a long iron. They are also pretty good out of reasonable lies in the rough.

• IRONS There are so many different irons available nowadays that it is difficult to know where to start when it comes to offering advice.

There are basically three different types of irons on the market: the peripherally weighted, cavity-backed clubs that have big heads and a large sweet-spot, which are ideal for mid-to-high-handicap golfers; the old-fashioned blades, which are still the choice of some Tour professionals but are unforgiving and difficult to use; and the modern shallow-cavity irons that offer a compromise between the two. This new breed of clubs is designed to be used by professionals and low-handicap amateurs. They offer the benefits of peripheral weighting but tend to be smaller and less offset than the clubs in the cavity-backed sector.

A good PGA professional will be able to show you clubs from all three sectors of the market. He will also be able to give you advice on whether to use steel or graphite shafts in your irons. Historically, it was said that steel shafts offered more control than graphite shafts, but it could be argued that this is no longer the case. However, I believe that steel shafts still offer more 'feel' than graphite, which is why I still use them in my irons.

• PUTTERS Choosing a putter is all about finding a club that feels right. It is as simple, or as difficult, as that. In some hands, a £200 putter will work wonders. In others, a £20 model will work just as well, or better. Some golfers go for years without switching putters, while others change almost every time they have a bad putting round. I would recommend that if you are putting well, you should stick with what you have got. However, if you are struggling, try something different.

WHY YOU NEED A SPECIALIST WEDGE

You might have noticed that over the last four or five years there has been a significant trend towards Tour professionals carrying what can be described as 'specialist' wedges.

Nowadays, almost all Tour pros carry at least three wedges. Some have even gone one stage further and have added a fourth to the bag.

Personally, I think it makes a lot of sense to have a 'specialist' wedge at your disposal. Sometimes, of course, the pitching wedge from your set of irons will suffice for the shot you face. But, at other times, when you have to play a delicate lob, or a shot over trees, something different is required.

I believe most handicap golfers should opt for carrying three wedges and would recommend that you went for an additional wedge that fills the gap between your pitching wedge and your sand wedge.

Given that, nowadays, pitching wedges have about 48 degrees of loft and sand wedges have about 56 degrees of loft, what you should be looking for is a club with about 52 degrees of loft.

I should add that I would be a little bit wary about opting for one of those new lob wedges that have up to 60 degrees of loft. The simple fact is that they are not easy to use. They require good technique and confidence in equal measure. Phil Mickelson might be able to use them but not many others can, I'm afraid.

BE PREPARED

Sometimes, when I am playing in pro-ams, I am asked why it is that Tour professionals make their caddies carry such big bags. I explain that it is not just to keep our sponsors happy, although that is an important consideration, but also to give us plenty of room to store all the bits and pieces we might need during the course of a round.

When I go out to play a competitive round, I make sure I am prepared for almost every eventuality. I am well aware that, in changeable weather or in emergency situations, the other contents of my golf bag can be almost as important as my clubs. For that reason, just in case it rains, I never step onto the course without an umbrella, my waterproofs, a club cover, spare towels and two or three extra gloves. Seldom, except in the most benign climatic conditions, do I go out without a spare sweater or slipover.

Many people are surprised to see how much stuff is stored in my bag. In addition to my wet-weather gear and the usual stock of tees, pencils and ball markers, I carry a small emergency kit containing a cleat-tightening tool, spare cleats, sun cream, a Swiss Army knife, a groove cleaner, aspirin, plasters, antiseptic cream and insect repellent. Invariably, before we go out, we also stock up with water, bananas and other fruit, even though, at Tour events, we know that we will find all of those things on most tees out on the course.

SHOULD YOU GET YOUR CLUBS FITTED?

Once there was a time when 99 per cent of amateur golfers would walk into a professional shop and buy their clubs straight off the shelf. The chances were that they would have no more than four or five different sets to chose from. Left-handed golfers would probably have a good deal less.

Fortunately, things have moved on a bit since then. Most shops now offer customers a much wider range of products to chose from. Many also offer a custom fit service, at least for some of the products they stock.

Manufacturers, fitters and retailers are almost unanimous in agreeing that nearly everybody will benefit from custom fitting, although it has to be said that low handicappers, with sound, repeatable swings, will probably gain most from the process. In contrast, if you are a higher handicapper, who has a less grooved swing, you might not get quite as much out of a custom fitting session. However, even then, it is probably still worth considering, particularly as it takes no more than 30–45 minutes and is invariably fun as well.

If you do decide to go through the process, I think you will be surprised to find just how much the set-up of your clubs can influence the shape of your shots. Lie angle, shaft length, loft, shaft flex and grip size will all have a direct bearing on how well, or badly, you hit the ball. Get one, or more, of them wrong, and you will never maximise your potential.

Lie angle, for example, is crucial, because if your clubs are too flat (see below centre), it could exacerbate your hook. Conversely, if your clubs are too upright (see below right), you will slice more than you would have done. Your club should sit nicely on the ground as shown (see below left). When lying correctly you should be able to squeeze a ten pence coin under the toe, but that is about all.

Similarly, choosing the correct shaft flex is also vital. If your shots fly low and tail off to the right, the chances are your existing shafts are too stiff for you. Conversely, if your shots soar heavenwards and then move to the left in the air, you might want to test stiffer shafts.

A well-trained club fitter will offer you advice in both these areas. He will also examine the size of your hands to see if you should be using thin, standard or thick grips. Again, this will have important repercussions on how you perform on the course. If your grips are too thin for you, your hands could get over-active and a hook will result. In contrast, if your grips are too thick, you won't be able to use your hands effectively and you will almost certainly slice the ball.

LOOK AFTER YOUR CLUBS

Many of you, it would seem, are quite prepared to part with £1,000 to buy a set of clubs but then let them deteriorate through lack of care and attention.

Playing in pro-ams, I have lost count of the number of times I have seen amateurs using clubs that are so dirty that you can hardly see the grooves. Invariably, the same people comment on how much I can spin the ball, completely oblivious to the fact that without clean grooves not even Tiger Woods could create backspin.

I recommend that all golfers should get into the habit of cleaning their clubs after each round they play. It doesn't take much. All it needs is a cloth and a bit of soap and water, although you could also invest in one of those specialist groove cleaners that many PGA professionals stock.

While on the subject of maintaining your clubs, it is also important to change your grips from time to time as shiny, worn ones will undoubtedly have a detrimental effect on your performance. Golf Pride, the world's No. I manufacturer of golf grips, recommends that regular golfers should change their grips every twelve months or so. If you practise a lot, you might even want to change them a little bit more often.

HOW TO CHOOSE THE RIGHT BALL FOR YOU

Golf balls might not look much different to what they used to but appearances can be deceptive. Over the last few years the major manufacturers have made sweeping changes in the way they design and construct their products and these changes mean that modern balls perform completely differently to their predecessors.

Ten years ago it would have been fair to say there were basically two types of golf ball on the market. There were the 'soft' balata balls that professionals and low-handicap amateurs used to maximise the spin they achieved around the greens, and there were 'hard' synthetic balls that amateurs preferred because they gave them a little more distance. The former were constructed in three pieces with a cover made from soft balata. The latter were made in two pieces with a central core surrounded by a durable outer cover.

Nowadays, however, things are not quite so simple. Balata, for a start, is basically obsolete, replaced by multi-layer balls designed to offer both distance and feel. The two-piece market has also fragmented, with the manufacturers offering both 'distance' and 'performance' two-piece products.

Basically, what has happened is that the manufacturers have found new ways to marry distance and feel. Once, not that long ago, the two were mutually exclusive. Now, thanks to new technology, you can get both, in varying degrees.

As a result of these changes, each golfer has to make up his own mind exactly what he wants from his golf ball. Does he want feel, spin or distance? More precisely, what combination of the three does he want?

Obviously, in the end, that comes down to personal choice but there are several general observations that can be made. If, for example, you rely heavily on your short game, the best choice for you will probably be one of the softer golf balls. Equally, if your golf course is hard and fast-running, you might opt for a soft ball because you will be able to stop it a little bit quicker.

At the other end of the spectrum, if you struggle for distance, or play on a wet golf course, you should probably plump for one of the 'distance' options. They will undoubtedly give you an extra yard or two, although the downside is that they don't offer much 'feel' around the greens.

Over the last few years, arguably the biggest changes have been made in what can be described as the middle ground. Nowadays, most manufacturers offer products that give a hitherto unobtainable combination of distance and control. This has proved to be a great development for good golfers, who like the idea of achieving greater distance but still place a premium on control. However, it has also meant that we have all had to experiment a bit more to find the ball we like best.

At the end of the day, technological advances have meant that the ball market has become somewhat confusing to the average golfer, as one leading manufacturer alluded to in a recent advertising campaign. That being the case, I suggest the best way forward is to have a chat with your local PGA professional. Tell him about the strengths and weaknesses of your game. Let him know what you want out of a golf ball and then try out the balls he recommends to see which ones you like best.

After that, I would suggest you stick with that ball, at least until the manufacturers come up with something better. I'm not advocating blind allegiance, which is the probably the manufacturers' goal, but, for consistency's sake, I do feel it's better to stick to one product, except, I suppose, in exceptional weather conditions. Certainly, using a soft ball on one hole and a hard one on another is asking for trouble, on and around the greens. It will also lead to club selection difficulties, which is the last thing you need.

There once was a time when it was thought that you did not have to be particularly fit to become a top Tour golfer. Back in the 1960s and 1970s, stories abounded about leading Tour stars burning the candle at both ends, but, nowadays, such tales are rare. Sure, most Tour golfers still like the odd tipple from time to time, but seldom during a competition and never to the detriment of their performance on the course.

Getting Fit for Golf

Over the last few years, many leading Tour golfers have adopted fitness regimes every bit as rigorous as those undertaken by swimmers, footballers, rugby players and athletes, and there is no doubt that their improved levels of fitness have enhanced their performances. Coming to the end of 2003, it is abundantly clear that top Tour golfers now hit the ball considerably further than they have ever done before, and that is certainly not all down to improvements in technology and course maintenance. Likewise, modern Tour stars also seem to possess much more stamina, even in oppressively hot climates, another sure sign that their cardiovascular fitness is far better than that of their predecessors.

While few readers will have either the time or indeed the inclination to work as hard in the gym as Tiger Woods, the good news is that even a slight improvement in your level of fitness and flexibility can enhance your performance on the golf course. Take it from me; I know.

FLEXIBILITY IS THE KEY

When I sat down to think about this chapter on fitness, the one word that kept springing to mind was 'flexibility'. I firmly believe that all golfers could improve their game if they worked on increasing their flexibility, and I should know because I have experienced the process at first hand.

Many readers will know that at the start of 2002 I suffered a serious back injury that forced me to pull out of several events Down Under. Despite receiving treatment, I was to continue to have problems for much of the year, at one time even thinking that I might have to pull out of the Ryder Cup because of the pain.

Back problems, as we all know, are quite common in the game of golf. If you take ten guys who play golf regularly, it could well be that four, or even five, of them have the same problem as me. This is partly due to the fact that the golf swing is a pretty unnatural movement. However, it goes much deeper than that. In my case, and for many others, it was exacerbated by the fact that I was overweight and not as fit as I should have been.

When I went to see a specialist, he was quick to isolate the problem, telling me that, in the short term at least, the only cure was to rest and recuperate. However, taking things a stage further, he also warned me that I would continue to experience difficulties unless I did something about my overall fitness and flexibility. Put bluntly, he told me my golf career was in danger of coming to a premature end unless I lost weight and improved my fitness level. When confronted by these facts, a professional sportsman has a stark choice: either he does what he is told, or else he finds another job.

I love playing golf for a living so, for me, there was no choice to make. Quickly, I enlisted the help of a fitness trainer and a dietician. Both, I was told, would be vital if I was to cure my back problem. I learned that shedding weight was important, because excess weight increases the pressure on your back. But losing the pounds solves only 50 per cent of the problem. To alleviate it further, you need to exercise to strengthen the muscles that stabilise the spine. You also have to work on your overall flexibility, something that decreases as you age, unless you do something about it.

The good news is that, more than a year later, I am still following the advice I received. I have lost weight and stuck to my exercise regime, and, consequently, I had few back problems in 2003. Sometimes, of course, I felt the odd twinge or two, but that is hardly surprising, given the amount of practice I do.

The sound advice I received from the experts is applicable to most other golfers, too. One expert I spoke to was brutally frank about the scale of the problem. 'Golfers' bodies often end up in a bit of a mess,' he told me. 'Their physical problems related to playing the game get worse the more they play and the older they get unless they take avoiding action, which few of them seem to do. Very few golfers look after their bodies and maintain their flexibility. If they work out at all, it's to increase strength, not flexibility. That's dangerous, and is bound to lead to problems.' As that is the case, it seems to me that you have to do *something*. The only real question is how much?

In an ideal world, I would suggest you should go to a local gym and get a trained fitness instructor to map out a complete training programme for you. A programme of this sort will include exercises designed to increase your core strength, developing strong muscles in your stomach and lower back. It will also include cardiovascular training and exercises to increase your flexibility. Of course, if you do not have access to a fitness trainer, you could opt to try to plan a programme for yourself. If that is the route you choose, I suggest you start by assessing your own strengths and weaknesses. For example, if the main priority is to lose weight, plan on doing a lot of cardiovascular exercise. Conversely, if improved strength is the objective, spend more time on that area. Whatever you do, when planning a fitness programme, remember to be realistic. There is no point planning daily two-hour workouts if your lifestyle does not allow you the time to do this.

At the very least, even if you do not want to embark on a fitness programme, all golfers owe it to themselves to get into the habit of warming up properly before each round of golf. For some reason, many golfers seem loath to do this, which is nonsensical, given that you can considerably improve your chances of scoring well simply by ensuring that your muscles are warmed up before you reach the first tee.

As I have mentioned earlier, I set great store by warming up properly. Prior to hitting some shots, I will touch my toes, do side bends and various other loosening-up exercises (see panel) before continuing the process by swinging with two clubs. Next I proceed to hit some practice shots, starting with my wedge and working up to the driver. Only then will I move to the first tee.

HOW TO WARM UP FOR GOLF

Anyone who has been involved in golf for any length of time will know there are numerous exercises designed to help you warm up. Here are some of my favourites.

EXERCISE 1
Before leaving the locker room, get into the habit of doing what I call the 'Wall Drill'. Using a wall for support, stand as upright as you can, with your back, shoulder-blades and neck against the wall. Move your arms up so that your upper arms are parallel to the ground, your forearms are pointing upwards and the backs of your hands are against the wall. Now suck in your tummy, hold for twenty seconds, and then relax. Repeat three or four times. This exercise will get your spine in a good position and also stretch the muscles in the front of your body. It is particularly useful if you have spent all day driving or working in a sedentary position.

EXERCISES 2 AND 3
When you get out to the practice ground, continue to warm up by doing some side bends. Stand tall with your hands on your hips. Now bend slowly, first to the right and then to the left. Repeat several times, making sure you are bending from the hips. Once you have done this, proceed to touch your toes a few times. Try to keep your legs reasonably straight, but, whatever you do, don't try to force it.

EXERCISE 4
Place a club behind your neck so it is sitting on your shoulders, parallel to the ground. Put one hand close to the head and the other on the grip, and then turn your upper body slowly, first to the right and then to the left. Repeat the movement several times in both directions.

EXERCISE 5
Stand tall with your arms at your sides and with your hands holding a golf club horizontally across your thighs. From this starting position, slowly lift the club above your head, continuing until you feel your chest lifting and your back stretching. Return to the starting position and repeat three or four times.

Acknowledgements

I'D LIKE TO THANK THE FOLLOWING:

MY FAMILY (MY WIFE EIMEAR AND CHILDREN OLIVIA, VENETIA AND CAMERON)

COLIN CALLANDER FOR HIS GREAT HELP AND SUPPORT WITH THIS BOOK

MY COACHES DENIS PUGH, BILL FERGUSON AND PAUL MARCHAND

JOHN JACOBS, OBE

ORION (IAN PREECE, HARRY GREEN, PHILIP PARR AND ALAN SAMSON)

DAVE CANNON AND ANDY REDINGTON FROM GETTY IMAGES

ALL THE STAFF AT THE WESTIN TURNBERRY RESORT, WISLEY GOLF CLUB AND VALDERRAMA GOLF CLUB

IMG (IN PARTICULAR, JANE BROOKS, GUY KINNINGS, BRENDAN TAYLOR AND SARAH WOOLDRIDGE)